A
LOVING
TABLE

A LOVING TABLE

CREATING MEMORABLE GATHERINGS

KIMBERLY SCHLEGEL WHITMAN
AND SHELLEY JOHNSTONE PASCHKE

PRINCIPAL PHOTOGRAPHY BY JOHN CAIN SARGENT
FOREWORD BY MARK D. SIKES

GIBBS SMITH
TO ENRICH AND INSPIRE HUMANKIND

First Edition
25 24 23 22   4 3

End sheet art is a custom color of Ivory Silhouette, courtesy of Gracie Studio

Photographic credits on page 299
Back cover photos © 2022:
Top left from Kim Hersov, by Ingrid Rasmussen
Top right from Kimberly Schlegel Whitman, by John Cain Sargent
Bottom left from Penny Morrison, by Mike Garlick
Bottom right from Alessandra Branca, by Ana Lui

Published by
Gibbs Smith
P.O. Box 667
Layton, Utah 84041

1.800.835.4993 orders
www.gibbs-smith.com

Designed by Rita Sowins / Sowins Design
Printed and bound in China

Gibbs Smith books are printed on paper produced from sustainable PEFC-certified forest/controlled wood source. Learn more at www.pefc.org.

Library of Congress Control Number: 2021946775

ISBN: 978-1-4236-5761-3

To our mothers, Myrna and Vicki,
and all the women who have inspired and
influenced us to set a loving table.
And to our husbands, children, and extended families for your
endless support. You fill our lives and tables with laughter and joy.

CONTENTS

FOREWORD

MARK D. SIKES

GROWING UP, I SPENT NEARLY EVERY WEEKEND AS A YOUNG BOY WITH MY GRANDPARENTS IN MATTOON, ILLINOIS. Grandma always festooned the table in her lime-green kitchen with simple, grandmotherly touches: place mats in vibrant Pucci-esque hues; a throng of serving dishes for sundry leftovers; and a nosegay of weedy daisies plucked from her garden. Nothing was beautiful or rarefied in the aesthetic ways I champion as a designer now, yet I felt so much love and was so warmly welcomed into their home that those meals were among the most treasured I've ever had. I later dedicated my first book, *Beautiful*, to my grandparents.

My parents rarely entertained, but for our dinners as a family, they set a scene that intentionally matched the surrounding decor, running a natural fiber runner down the center of the table with woven rattan place mats and a powdery sky-blue striped tablecloth. (I dedicated my second book, *More Beautiful*, to my parents.)

I didn't learn about formal "entertaining" and hosting dinner parties until I was out on my own and developing my own style. One of my heroes: the ineffable Bunny Williams, whom I visited often at her home La Colina in Punta Cana, Dominican Republic, and in Falls Village, Connecticut. Bunny amazed me. At every single meal there was a different tablecloth, type of napkin, and floral arrangement. Her butler's pantry was fully stocked, with an entire wall of decorative objects; still more walls of dishes; and drawers upon drawers of finishing pieces like tablecloths, napkins, and napkin rings.

As I got older and started understanding more about entertaining and parties, I thought about the different types of dish collections we have in our own home and have made sure that we keep a drawer full of different tablecloths, with fine linens for the dining room and more boutique-y things for the buffets we often set up for guests at our kitchen island. But I firmly believe that as long as you're setting up your tablescapes with loving hands, you're doing it right.

Coming together with friends old and new for a meal is a tradition as ancient as humanity itself. It's less about having the latest Instagrammable flatware and more about the feelings and experiences you'll share, not to mention the memories and stories you'll take with you long after the leftovers are gone. So, I was thrilled to hear about Shelley Johnstone and Kimberly Whitman's new book, *A Loving Table*. Arranging memorable tablescapes for family and friends is something both Shelley and Kimberly truly cherish doing, which is evident on every single page of this book. They have gathered experiences and photographs of unforgettable gatherings hosted by dozens of unstoppable women, including my friends Alessandra Branca, Filipa de Abreu, and Fruzsina Keehn, whom I admire so much. Every page in the book is pure eye candy, and each fête is one I'd certainly RSVP yes to! I once had the pleasure of staying at Shelley's home in Lake Forest, Illinois, and spending time with her family. I don't recall the specific tablescape she arranged for each meal—although, of course, it was exquisite—but what I'll never forget is her overwhelming attention to detail that conjured a delightful experience for me.

I've always believed that beauty is everywhere, and that it will save the day—it's unequivocally a mood booster. That starts at home, whether you live in a Midwestern cottage or a private Caribbean compound. Setting a table beautifully has taken on new meaning recently, when the true importance of being together in person with friends and family came to light. Each moment we can spend together is a gift—and we should wrap it gorgeously! So, as we all come back together with our loved ones again, creative tablescapes that help inspire lasting memories are as key as the menu itself. (Plus, setting a table is so fulfilling. Like planning a much-anticipated trip, it brings so much joy.) When you're hosting friends and family, the care and thought that go into preparing something special for loved ones is what's really beautiful.

INTRODUCTION

IT IS HARD TO PUT INTO WORDS THE FEELING OF COMFORT THAT COMES WITH A FAMILIAR FAMILY SETTING AROUND A TABLE. Maybe it is the tastes, the smells, the sights, the sounds, or the touch of the familiar. There is just something magical about recreating the special touches that your mother, grandmother, godmother, or aunt employed when hosting a family get-together. Traditions add texture and infuse a unique flavor to any gathering and we wanted to celebrate that in this book, a collection of images, stories, ideas, and traditions from some of the most stylish women around the world.

You may smile when you open one of your grandmother's recipe books and see her notes in the margins in her signature flourished cursive. When you taste the sweet potatoes right out of the skillet, delectable with brown sugar and butter, on Thanksgiving and Christmas, memories of the same meal around tables filled with family might flood your thoughts. When you smell a rose-fragrance candle burning, maybe you think of your grandmother and her signature scent. When you see light bounce off an etched crystal goblet, you may reminisce about stories that were told around your mother's formal table. There is so much joy in the comfort of a family tradition.

Around the world, women celebrate the other women in their family through little nods when they entertain. This book is a tribute to all of the lessons we learned and styles we adopted from the women in our lives. When we set out to find the right women to include in this book, we were moved by all of the wonderful ways that these style-setters honored the women who came before them and added their own fresh spin on old family traditions. Carrying on a tradition doesn't mean that it needs to be done exactly the same way that it was done in the generations before. It is exciting to see how these women made inherited customs their own.

We hope this book and the women featured within its pages will inspire you to continue or start a family tradition of your own. We hope you will create memories with your loved ones through time around a table and let your personal style shine through.

KIMBERLY SCHLEGEL WHITMAN
AND SHELLEY JOHNSTONE PASCHKE

FRIENDSGIVING DINNER

ARIEL OKIN

Photographer: DONNA DOTAN

A luxury interior designer whose eponymous firm is based in New York, Ariel Okin fondly remembers growing up in a home where her parents loved to entertain. Her dad was an exceptional cook, and she learned from him about timing, plating, and presentation. Her mom always had beautiful, timeless floral arrangements throughout the house, even in the powder room. To this day, Ariel can hear her mother's heels clicking across the wood floors of her childhood home as she emerged dressed to the nines, smelling like Shalimar perfume, and ready to host a party.

After graduating from college and moving to New York City, Ariel missed the foods her parents served at home for Thanksgiving, so she started a new tradition of hosting her best girlfriends for a second Thanksgiving, where she would serve foods that reminds her of home: roast chicken, her father's famous sweet potato casserole, cornbread, and Parker House dinner rolls fresh from the oven, along with decadent pies from Four and Twenty Blackbirds. Now a wife and mother, Ariel still relishes her annual Friendsgiving gatherings, especially the all-night conversations with girlfriends! Her table is set with a charming mix of tableware, and there are always seasonal flowers.

Ariel feels really lucky to have two sets of family, on both her and her husband's sides, who really nail the beauty of getting people together, which, at the end of the day, is just about having fun. Her style is to entertain with a sense of ease and friendliness; she never wants anyone to feel like they don't know what fork to use at her table! Her emphasis is on good, home-cooked food, not too fussy, and bare feet are welcome!

OPPOSITE: A vintage suzani throw is used as a tablecloth and is topped with colored glass and china, bone-handled flatware, fresh fruit, and flowers, creating a charmingly layered table.

OVERLEAF LEFT: An eclectic mix of styles, from modern Italian glassware to Royal Copenhagen's 250-year-old Blue Fluted dinner plates, mingles with fruit and flowers on Ariel's Friendsgiving tablescape. OVERLEAF RIGHT: Off to the side, a wicker bar cart is party ready. The wallpaper is a hand-painted design by Gracie.

"When my parents and in-laws entertain (they are all great hosts),
it always feels special, but never precious.
Nothing is over the top, and it always feels like they went the extra mile to
make their guests feel welcome. That sense of ease is
something I aim to provide when hosting."
—ARIEL OKIN

OPPOSITE: Ariel's inspiration board is grounded by her own design for The Mural Source. THIS PAGE: The dining room is ready for the arrival of guests.

SWEET POTATO CASSEROLE

6 large sweet potatoes (about 1½ per person)

2 tablespoons milk or heavy cream, optional

Brown sugar, to taste

1 stick butter, melted

1 bag mini marshmallows

Pumpkin pie seasoning

Cinnamon

Preheat the oven to 350°F. Bake the sweet potatoes in a conventional oven until soft. When done, scoop out all meat into a large mixing bowl. Mash completely using a potato masher, fork, or hand mixer. Mix in the optional milk or heavy cream at this point for a little more richness.

In a 5-to-7-inch-high greased casserole dish, start with a 2-inch layer of potatoes, then sprinkle on a layer of brown sugar. Drizzle on a layer of melted butter until it coats the brown sugar then add a layer of marshmallows covering it all. Finish with a coating of pumpkin pie seasoning and cinnamon over the marshmallows.

Continue this same process until you are about 1 inch from the top of the dish with marshmallows and seasoning. A sprinkling of brown sugar is the last thing to put on top. Bake until bubbly (about 45 minutes). Keep a close watch not to let the topping burn. Excellent served with turkey, duck, or chicken.

SERVES 6–8

VIETNAMESE CHRISTMAS EVE

NAM DANG-MITCHELL

Photographer: NAM DANG-MITCHELL

Portrait by Hunter Mitchell

Christmas Eve is beautiful chaos at interior designer Nam Dang-Mitchell's home in Calgary, Alberta. The snow is always falling and her elegant natural décor is up around the door. But at the table, eating a family favorite, Garlic Ginger Fried Crab, can be a real mess, and they love it! Nam's family is all about food. They do a big traditional turkey dinner on Christmas Day, so the night before is reserved for a celebration of her family's favorite Vietnamese recipes.

Growing up, Nam begged her mother to make her famous Fried Crab. Her mother, Yvonne, is an inspiration to her in so many ways and has taught Nam the special recipe. Nam loves how preparing it makes her feel like a real grown-up, as preparing family recipes can do! She adds more red chili peppers than her mother's original recipe calls for, and the dish is her family's Christmas Eve tradition.

Nam's family is made up of creatives; they work in food, architecture, interior design, furniture making, real estate development, and floral design, so they have a natural team of talents when it comes to stylish family gatherings. Setting the table and making a special meal is a real art form for all of them, and they love to prepare together in advance and then attend their own party.

Nam says she "has learned that sharing food is at the heart of what it means to be a family. It is love and connection." Her family relishes the comforts of home and their particular family traditions at Christmastime. There is always more than enough and leftovers abound, as their family mantra is "More food!"

OPPOSITE: Every December, Nam and her family use natural evergreens and pine cones to decorate the front door of their Calgary, Alberta, home.

OPPOSITE: Cognac-colored leather dining chairs, pottery vases filled with fresh-cut pine branches and berries, candles, and an elegant crystal chandelier set the mood for a cozy Christmas Eve dinner.

ABOVE: A marble-topped gilt console in the dining room displays the thoughtful wine selections for the evening's meal.

YVONNE'S GARLIC GINGER
FRIED CRAB

*3¾ pounds of fresh crabs (approximately
2 large or 3 medium crabs)*

4 teaspoons sea salt

1 teaspoon freshly ground pepper

1 cup all-purpose flour

½ cup vegetable oil, for frying

*1 large yellow onion, diced and divided
(reserve 2 tablespoons for sauce)*

*¼ cup minced fresh garlic, divided
(reserve 1 teaspoon for sauce)*

*¼ cup peeled, julienned fresh ginger, divided
(reserve 1 teaspoon for sauce)*

½ bunch green onions, cut into 1-inch pieces

¼ cup fresh cilantro for garnish

THE SAUCE

2 teaspoons vegetable oil

2 tablespoons reserved chopped onion

1 teaspoon reserved minced garlic

1 teaspoon reserved julienned ginger

Yellow fat from the crab shells

1½ teaspoons sugar

1 teaspoon sea salt

Ground pepper to taste

2 serrano chiles, minced, optional

Rice or French bread for serving

When you buy the crabs, have the vendor cut them into quarters for you. Make sure they give you the carapace (back shell), which contains the yellow fat. You will need it for the sauce.

Break down the crab pieces lightly with a mallet so they will be easier to eat later. Remove the yellow fat from all the shells and set it aside. Clean out one shell for presentation on the dish.

Season the crab pieces with salt and pepper and toss them in flour.

Prepare a large frying pan or wok with vegetable oil (medium-to-high heat). Fry the flour-coated crab pieces and the one cleaned shell (no flour) to cook them slightly, 10 minutes. Take these partially cooked crab pieces out of the wok and set them aside. Leave the wok with the oil in it; you will use it again.

Prepare the sauce: In a small saucepan over medium heat, add the vegetable oil, diced onion, minced garlic, and julienned ginger. Let it brown; then add the yellow fat, stirring well. Add sugar, sea salt, and ground pepper to taste. The sauce should thicken after a few minutes.

In the wok you put aside, add the rest of the onion, garlic, and ginger and sauté on medium-high heat until they soften. Add the crab pieces back in, along with the optional serrano chiles, and toss all together. Lower the heat and add the sauce you prepared. Cook for another 7–10 minutes, mixing so the crab is well coated. Finally, add the cut green onions and put a lid over the wok for 3 minutes to turn them a bright green. Add a little water if the sauce sticks to the bottom of the pan.

Scoop it all onto a big platter, place the shell artfully, and add cilantro to garnish. Serve with rice or French bread and lots of napkins! It is a messy, sticky finger treat! Pairs well with a crisp white wine.

SERVES 4

"It is unforgivable in Vietnamese culture to
not serve enough food,
so there are always leftovers at our house."
—*NAM DANG-MITCHELL*

RIGHT: Nam's mother, Yvonne Nhan.

MARDI GRAS
BRUNCH

JULIE NEILL

Photographer: ALISON GOOTEE / Stylist: SUZONNE STIRLING

When it comes to mother-daughter brunches, nothing could be more festive than the annual Mardi Gras gathering hosted by Julie Neill and her daughter Isabelle Neill at their Garden District home in New Orleans. The stage is set just steps away from the traditional parade route on St. Charles Avenue, creating the perfect place to enjoy the festivities from morning until night.

This dynamic duo work well together, whether in Julie's eponymous lighting design company or planning each and every detail of a party. They love putting their talents together to plan food and decorations for multiple generations of their family and friends.

Julie's grandmother Rose was Sicilian and loved to cook. She cherished large family dinners and was happiest watching her friends and family enjoying her beautiful meals! Growing up, Julie loved to help her cook and set the table with family silver, linens, and flowers. They still use many of those treasures today, including the recipes! Making them is special because Julie feels that her granny would be so happy to know that generations are carrying on these great family traditions.

Julie's other grandmother, Dorothy, loved all aspects of entertaining, except that she didn't cook herself. She loved to research recipes and plan wonderful meals but preferred having help to make them. She had an incredible eye for beauty and made sure every detail of her table was perfect. Her collection of china was vast and her passion for beautiful florals was evident in every room of her house. Julie was Dorothy's first granddaughter, and when she was born she was gifted a set of pink Minton china that started Julie off on a lifetime of collecting. Today, Julie and Isabelle love to mix and match the Minton with other collections in various ways.

Both of Julie's grandmothers taught her that beauty is in the details and that a host can never have enough well-prepared food presented in a beautiful way. Isabelle shares this sentiment and cherishes the tradition of collaborating with her mother to create the scene for memorable gatherings.

OPPOSITE: A whimsical tablecloth of Carnival Toile fabric by Palm Orleans sets the tone for the Neill family's annual Mardi Gras brunch.

"From both of my grandmothers I learned that beauty is in the details and special touches make the party."
—*JULIE NEILL*

OPPOSITE AND ABOVE: Julie's pink Minton china was a gift from her grandmother on the day she was born. She mixes it beautifully here with fresh linens, flowers, and champagne for brunch. Every detail of this brunch is a nod to the traditions of New Orleans Mardi Gras celebrations.

ABOVE: A mixed-media paper collage on canvas by Julie Neill hangs above a marble-topped console that displays Mardi Gras treasures. The white ceramic candlesticks with flower are by New Orleans artist Lisa Alpaugh. The female bust is dressed up for the occasion, wearing Mardi Gras colors and a crown with ostrich feathers. The crown, an icon of the tradition being celebrated, is found throughout the décor at the Neill house.

OPPOSITE: Purple, green, and gold blown-glass orbs fill a compote from Shadyside Pottery. These traditional Mardi Gras colors perfectly complement the Kent Walsh painting behind them.

GRANNY'S
BREAD PUDDING

1 loaf French bread (1½ feet long, 1 pound)

1 quart milk

3 eggs, beaten

2 cups sugar

2 tablespoons vanilla

1 teaspoon cinnamon

3 tablespoons butter

In a large bowl, break bread into bite-size pieces. Cover with milk and soak for 1 hour. Preheat oven to 375°F. Mix well. Add eggs and sugar. Stir in vanilla and cinnamon. Melt butter in a 13-by-9-by-2-inch baking dish, tilting to coat all sides. Pour in the pudding and bake 1 hour.

SAUCE

1 stick (½ cup) butter

1 cup sugar

1 egg, beaten

¼ cup bourbon

In the top of a double boiler, melt butter and sugar. Gradually whisk in egg and cook until mixture thickens. Cool slightly. Add bourbon. If serving right away, pour warm sauce over pudding. If not, warm the sauce slightly before serving and serve it in a sauce boat.

SERVES 12

35

BACKYARD
END-OF-SUMMER DINNER

SHELLEY JOHNSTONE PASCHKE

Photographer: CYNTHIA LYNN KIM

Shelley Johnstone Paschke is a natural when it comes to entertaining. She looks no further than her own cupboards and garden when setting the table. Because most of the things she loves work well together, she is able to pull a table together with little forethought or planning, either at home in Lake Forest, Illinois, or at the family's winter getaway in Naples, Florida. Her own garden is full of fresh florals and ingredients for the meal as well.

Shelley's mother, Vicki, was a florist, and Shelley grew up helping her mom both in her floral shop and at home in her beautiful gardens. Her mother also started the tradition of setting the table no matter what the occasion was. She had a fluid ease for designing the table, from the layers of linens to the lovely floral arrangements. Everything was "simple yet interesting" and Shelley has now brought that into her own home, emulating the warm and inviting environment that her mother established.

Growing up with creative parents means that gardening and design have been a part of Shelley's everyday life as long as she can remember. As an interior designer with a showroom, Shelley continues to be surrounded by inspiration every day. She has curated a wonderful collection of entertaining pieces that she keeps orga-

nized behind her jib-door cabinets. "I set a lot of tables both inside and outdoors for my large crew; having it all right there keeps it easy and fun."

Shelley's family enjoys pulling from the vegetable and herb garden in their backyard to make a meal. Her husband, Brett, who also grew up with a garden at home, is their "head gardener." Her daughter-in-law, Sophie, is adding a new element to their family traditions by bringing her culinary skills to the table. For the end-of-summer dinner offered here, Sophie added recipes from her family. She is a perfect addition to Shelley's family, as she often says, "You go set the table and I'll prepare the meal!" Everyone gets to put their talents to use for making the family gatherings memorable occasions.

In addition to the traditional recipes that Sophie is sharing with her new family, Shelley's family cherishes a flourless chocolate cake recipe on special occasions. The recipe was shared with them over twenty years ago on a trip to Capri, Italy, and her entire family takes part in its preparation. With Shelley and her mother effortlessly decorating the table and Sophie in the kitchen preparing family recipes, a dinner at the Paschke house is full of fresh takes on family traditions.

PREVIOUS OVERLEAF LEFT: Shelley Johnstone Paschke with her mother, Vicki.
PREVIOUS OVERLEAF RIGHT: Dishes are from Penny Morrison. LEFT: A summer table nestled among an allée of Bradford Pear trees creates a casual and inviting outdoor setting. Pink-and-white chair cushions us well as pink and green hues of the garden influenced the colors chosen for the table.

"Our family table is our
happy place—a place where
we make memories.
It truly is a loving table.
To us it really is that simple.
With our large crew, every meal
around our table feels special."
—*SHELLEY JOHNSTONE PASCHKE*

ABOVE: The family enjoys a beautiful summer evening.
OPPOSITE TOP: Hellebores, peonies, garden roses, and jasmine vine arranged in straw baskets by Lord & Mar, Ltd, in Lake Forest, Illinois, add a divine scent.

OPPOSITE BOTTOM: Details of the table include a tablecloth with appliqué flowers from Elizabeth Lake and bamboo-style flatware. Penny Morrison dishes look splendid layered on woven chargers from Creel & Gow and accented with pink fringe napkins from Courtland & Co. Glasses are from Cabana Capri.

ABOVE: Food is arranged buffet style on a tablecloth by Mrs.
Alice. Tomatoes, basil, and other herbs were gathered from
the garden.
OPPOSITE: Sophie, Shelley's daughter-in-law, helps serve her
delicious meal.

TORTA CAPRESE FLOURLESS CHOCOLATE CAKE

9 ounces good quality dark chocolate, chopped into small pieces

1 cup butter

¼ cup cocoa powder

1 teaspoon almond extract

1¼ cups granulated sugar

1½ cups finely ground blanched and toasted almonds

6 medium-sized eggs, room temperature

Powdered sugar for dusting

Preheat oven to 310°F and line the bottom of a 9-inch springform pan with parchment paper.

Slowly melt the chocolate and butter over a double boiler. In a stand mixer with a whisk attachment, whisk together the melted chocolate mixture, cocoa powder, almond extract, and sugar until combined.

Add the ground almonds and whisk until combined. Add the eggs one at a time, adding each egg after the first has been incorporated into the mixture. Pour mixture into the springform pan. Make sure the mixture is level and smooth on top. Bake for about 50 minutes. The cake will rise a bit and then fall back on itself once it cools. The baking time varies slightly depending on your oven, but the cake should be very moist in the center and dense once it cools. Cool before serving and dust the top with powdered sugar. Buon appetito!

SERVES 8

MOTHER'S DAY BRUNCH

CHESIE BREEN

Photographer: TRIA GIOVAN

Chesie Breen is a busy New York public relations executive who truly knows how to gather a meal together, although she may not often be found in the kitchen and admits she doesn't really enjoy cooking. She learned how to resource from one of the best as she watched her maternal grandmother spend an entire day driving considerable distances to pick up the finest pies, cakes, and savories from the very best sources in her close-knit community. She always knew who had the best ham, coconut cake, freshly grown strawberries, or hand-embroidered linens and would drive from house to house collecting things before a gathering.

Chesie acquired her passion for collecting from her mother, who has beautiful collections of porcelain, majolica, and vintage glassware and silver. Chesie's three daughters have amassed quite the collections of their own. At their christenings, each was gifted their first pieces of a Tiffany silver flatware collection, and they have been given additional pieces over the years. Her daughter Virginia now collects American Garden, Eliza received the Audubon pattern, and Margaret Ivy is accumulating Chrysanthemum.

Setting the table for friends and family using her collections gives Chesie joy. She tells her daughters she will pool their silver collections together for their weddings. They laugh and think she is joking, but she truly plans to do it, believing that the finest things should be used frequently and certainly on special occasions. It is these little things that make experiences go from ordinary to extraordinary!

Chesie has inherited and acquired more than just collections for the table. Her house rules for entertaining include using coupes in favor of flutes for champagne, starting every gathering with an empty dishwasher, and having fun with a smile! She always prefers to heat and serve a meal so that all of the preparation is done in advance. And she never experiments with guests, preferring to serve tried-and-true menus that are always crowd-pleasers.

As a child, Chesie was included in party preparations, and she includes her daughters in the same way. Her mother has a natural talent with flowers and plants and, as Chesie puts it, can "spin magic" with them! Chesie takes time with her daughters to plan everything from menus to what to wear, just as she did when she was growing up. Her daughters are especially fond of planning a luncheon for Mother's Day, and Chesie adores spending the day celebrating them and imagining when they will become mothers.

PREVIOUS OVERLEAF: Vintage shell plates from KRB New York were a graduation gift for Chesie's daughter Eliza.
ABOVE: The Breens' handsome dining room boasts Gracie hand-painted wallpaper. The centerpiece is by Christopher Spitzmiller.

OPPOSITE TOP LEFT: Chesie's daughter Margaret Ivy's Tiffany Chrysanthemum silver looks lovely mixed with vintage fish forks from Ireland. The silver julep cup is from her daughter Virginia's christening and features her custom monogram and the date.
OPPOSITE TOP RIGHT: An antique white pitcher filled with daffodils.
OPPOSITE BOTTOM LEFT: Embroidered linens are by Nina Campbell.

"No one is impressed by how
fancy things are.
They only remember how
it felt to be there and how nice
it was to be invited."
—*CHESIE BREEN*

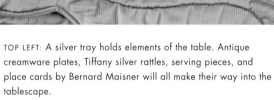

TOP LEFT: A silver tray holds elements of the table. Antique creamware plates, Tiffany silver rattles, serving pieces, and place cards by Bernard Maisner will all make their way into the tablescape.

BOTTOM LEFT: A breakfast tray is set with vintage applique and cross-stitch linens, Haviland Limoges, and an Irish Belleek creamer with clovers.

ABOVE RIGHT: Chesie's monogrammed linens were a gift from Ashley Whitaker and the glass bowl was a gift from Alex Papachristidis.

OPPOSITE: A silver gallery tray set with vintage champagne coupes is ready for guests. Flowers are arranged in a majolica pitcher.

EASTER ENTERTAINING
TRADITIONS

KIMBERLY SCHLEGEL WHITMAN

Photographer: JOHN CAIN SARGENT

Easter is a favorite holiday for Kimberly Whitman, a lifestyle expert and founder of ShopKSW.com. On Sunday, the extended family gathers at church and then meets at one of their homes for the traditional meal, always with the same menu and recipes that have been passed down from her mother and grandmother.

Setting the table with attention to detail is a trait that Kimberly learned from the women before her. Her mother and both of her grandmothers collected porcelain and pretty things for the table, and Kimberly was bitten by the same bug. She and her daughter, Millie, along with her mother, Myrna Schlegel, delight in setting the table together. Meaningful pieces—like the eggs Kimberly has collected on travels or received as gifts, the hand-painted flatware that her mother gave her, and the plates with the Whitman family monogram, gifted from her mother-in-law and hand-painted by family friend Joy de Rohan-Chabot—are arranged to make an enchanting table. Sugar diorama eggs are special gifts to the children each year, placed at their seats.

As prelude to Easter Sunday, the Whitmans and Schlegels host an Easter egg hunt for friends and family on Saturday at their family retreat, White Oaks Ranch, an hour outside of Dallas. The egg hunts began when Kimberly's son, JR, was only a few years old as a way to share the special holiday with JR's friends. Her parents also invited their friends with grandchildren, and for a number of years now, generations have gathered to enjoy the outdoors and renew friendships.

Over time, the extended family has grown and the guest list has gotten longer, which is all great with Kimberly! The party starts with a greeting from the Easter Bunny, who leads the way to the party pavilion, where food and drink are served. After a bit of mingling, music, and munchies, the little guests are gathered onto the steps of the pavilion to listen to someone special to the Whitman children—a treasured teacher, a godmother, or their grandfather—read a children's version of the biblical Easter story. The egg hunt follows, with the littlest guests being divided from the older ones so everybody can find candy for their baskets.

The children's joy combined with family union around the dinner table makes Easter a truly fulfilling holiday for Kimberly.

PREVIOUS OVERLEAF: A moss-covered basket holding blooming branches takes center stage on Kimberly's family table set for an Easter celebration. Hand-painted eggs rain down on the table. Their detailed designs delight adults and children alike.

ABOVE: Meaningful pieces grace the table. Detailed sugar diorama eggs are for the children. Porcelain-handled flatware hand-painted by Anna Weatherly was a gift from Kimberly's mother. The glass plates with the family monogram were hand-painted by family friend Joy de Rohan-Chabot. The embroidered tablecloth and napkins are D. Porthault. Cut crystal goblets are by Moser.

ABOVE: Kimberly; daughter, Millie; sisters, Krystal Davis and Kari Klower; and mother, Myrna Schlegel, all enjoy collaborating for family celebrations.
OVERLEAF: On the table, hand-painted porcelain eggs by Ginori 1735 are symbols of rebirth and hope.

ABOVE: Kimberly's dining room, lacquered in Persian Melon, is ready for her family. A custom-made table and Georgian chairs are at home with modern artwork by Tam van Tran and Matt Connors.
OPPOSITE, TOP LEFT: A delicate egg is decorated with cross-stitch and hand-painted flowers. TOP RIGHT: The three-dimensional painted flowers and Easter motifs are a topic of conversation around the Easter table.
BOTTOM LEFT: Place cards are by Patmos Plume; the hand-painted porcelain-handled spoon is by Anna Weatherly. BOTTOM RIGHT: Sugar diorama eggs are gifted to the children every year and placed at their seats at the table.

"My parents taught me that every good thing in life is a cause for celebration."
—*KIMBERLY SCHLEGEL WHITMAN*

Scenes from the annual Easter egg hunt that Kimberly's family hosts at their ranch outside of Dallas. Azaleas in moss-covered baskets are later replanted around the property. A petting zoo, snacks, and candy-filled eggs bring smiles and delight.

BABY'S BASTILLE DAY BIRTHDAY

CATHY KINCAID

Photographer: HOLT HAYNSWORTH

When interior designer Cathy Kincaid's granddaughter Margot was born on Bastille Day, a new tradition was begun. Margot's future birthdays would be celebrated in French style in honor of the fourteenth of July. For Margot's first birthday, Cathy hosted a garden party for three generations, including Margot's mother, Maggie Kincaid McMordie, and Alice Pate, the daughter of Maggie's best friend, Samantha Pate.

Outdoors at her home in Highland Park, Texas, Cathy decorated a table with the D. Porthault French linens that she has collected for many years. Margot's sweet little dress matched the pink and white Coeurs linens that D. Porthault first designed in the 1950s for the Duchess of Windsor.

The family's collection of antique silver baby cups that had been given to each of Cathy's four children were used for the special occasion alongside an antique Quimper tea set, also made in France. Julep cups were filled with pink and white peonies, hyacinths, and French tulips by Margaret Ryder of Fleurt Design. To bring memories of visits to France to the table, a souvenir Eiffel Tower was included, and the menu consisted of fleur-de-lis-shaped egg salad sandwiches, strawberries, and poodle sugar cookies made by master caterer Joanne Korges.

Cathy's masterful eye for color is important in her life and work. She was influenced by her mother and grandmother, who was part American Indian and had an extraordinary sense of color. Cathy's mother wisely taught her to celebrate imperfections and to live by the motto, "If you seek only perfect friends, you won't have any."

Cathy hopes that her new tradition of a Bastille Day birthday celebration at home will be a lovely reminder of how lucky we all are to have one another.

OPPOSITE: According to the celebrated French linen house D. Porthault, their classic Trèfles pattern symbolizes faith, hope, and good fortune. The linen is ideal for a Bastille Day birthday celebration. OVERLEAF: Souvenirs from French travels, pink peonies, and heirloom silver lend the ambience of France in Cathy Kincaid's backyard garden.

"If you seek only perfect friends, you won't have any."
—CATHY KINCAID

OPPOSITE AND ABOVE: An antique Quimper tea set and the
family's silver baby cups filled with flowers add a sentimental
touch to the table.

ROYAL LUNCHEON
IN PORTUGAL

DIANA DE CADAVAL

Photographer: JOÃO LIMA

The 11th Duchess de Cadaval, H.R.H. Princess Diana d'Orléans comes from a long line of women who entertained often. She certainly has many beautiful spaces to entertain in Portugal, whether it is the Cadaval Palace in Évora that has been in her family for over 600 years, in her contemporary home, or outdoors under the blue Portuguese sky. Although her family has a rich and fascinating history, Diana credits her mother, the Dowager Duchess de Cadaval, for inspiring her to be contemporary. Diana's mother has mastered the art of keeping tradition alive in their family but also keeps everything updated.

Diana believes that the most important quality a hostess can have is a welcoming tenderness and warm greeting that makes guests feel at home. She takes time to make introductions and invest in each person's experience, making sure they are comfortable as her guests.

Setting the table with style is something Diana is passionate about. Although her mother consistently uses elegant white flowers for every occasion, Diana is the queen of color. She adores classic color combinations of blue and white or green and white. On her tables, she gracefully and naturally combines antique family heirlooms with her mother's vintage collections and her own modern pieces. Diana's young daughter, Princess Isabelle, loves to set the table with abundant color too.

In addition to designing lovely tablescapes, Diana also aims to master the art of atmosphere through lighting. She knows firsthand that an evening can feel magical if the lighting is right and that low candle votives are the perfect way to add a flattering light to ladies' faces and jewels!

Diana's recipe for a successful gathering includes elements that fit as easily in a palace as they do in a garden. A warm greeting, flattering candlelight, and a beautiful tablescape are universally inviting.

PREVIOUS OVERLEAF AND THIS PAGE: Diana's table in the garden
is elegant, with Portuguese cabbage ware from Bordallo Pinheiro/
Vista Alegre, a printed tablecloth, and natural charger plates.
The green glasses are Biot, and the butterfly etched glasses are
Valentino Piu. White caned chairs provide comfortable seating in
the light and airy garden.

"Magic can happen if you really know how
to master your room lighting.
Add low candles to favor the best of ladies'
faces and jewels!"
— *DIANA DE CADAVAL*

ABOVE: The dining room is covered in blue and white *azulejos*
Portuguese tiles. The painting, by Rigaud, features the French side
of Diana's family. Chairs are 18th-century Portuguese antiques.
OPPOSITE: The plates, designed by Hubert de Givenchy and
custom made as a wedding gift for Diana's parents, the Duke and
Duchess de Cadaval, feature the ducal monogram and were made
in Provence. The glasses are from Dior. The elegant silverware
was a wedding gift to Diana's grandfather.

Mottahedeh Tobacco Leaf porcelain is made in Portugal by Vista Alegre. The tureen and place settings are exquisitely accented with D. Porthault napkins and heirloom candlesticks.

SUNDAY SUPPERS

DARA CAPONIGRO

Photographer: MAX KIM-BEE

Dara Caponigro lives life surrounded by talented creatives, and she is certainly one herself. As the creative director of Schumacher, one of the leading interior design sources in the U.S., Dara sees it all! She exudes an elegant and understated chic in all that she does, including the way she entertains. Her relaxed Sunday suppers at home in Fieldston, the Bronx, are filled with family and friends, quality food, and a bucolic atmosphere.

During Dara's youth, her mother hosted Sunday suppers that included extended family. The children were not allowed to see friends on Sundays, as the day was devoted to dining with relatives only! Her mother, an interior designer who was constantly educating herself on her favorite culinary passions, would start cooking around 9:00 in the morning, and the aunts, uncles, cousins, and grandparents would start arriving around 2:00 in the afternoon. There was always a pasta dish followed by a second course with meats and vegetables. The salad course came third and was followed by decadent desserts.

Dara's mother didn't stop at Italian cuisine, though. She took classes in French and Chinese cooking and made many things from scratch. Dara recalls her mother's attempt at homemade gnocchi, which she ruined by accidentally leaving the freezer open, turning all of the little dumplings into one big ball of mush! Her mother shared her gift for cooking by hosting frequent fancy dinner parties. Dara loved helping her by setting the table and even cleaning up.

Dara's fond memories of her family's Sunday suppers inspire her to replicate the experience with her own family today. Although she doesn't limit the guest list to family, she does want her guests to feel completely at home. She likes to host relaxed meals where, just as she remembers, guests arrive early in the day and enjoy an afternoon cooking, catching up, and relaxing together. She makes sure there is lots of room for conversation between courses and a sense of lingering that doesn't fit into a weeknight meal.

Instead of preparing every morsel of her meals from scratch, Dara prefers to supplement with high-quality, store-bought dishes. She steers away from outside help like servers or bartenders and prefers to keep the vibe casual and homey. And, just like her mother allowed her to help in the cleanup, she takes her guests up on their offers to help and clean up together, creating memories around a kitchen sink or having a fulfilling conversation while putting things away.

An inviting courtyard is the setting for dinner al fresco with friends.

ABOVE: A neutral Moroccan tablecloth is backdrop for Dara's
collection of dramatic green porcelain. The elegant armchairs are
from Formations.
OPPOSITE: Hand-painted pasta bowls by Carolina Irving & Daughters,
Georg Jensen silverware, and napkins made from F. Schumacher
& Co's Rania Stripe set a relaxed and interesting scene.

"You can't always expect to have fun yourself if you're orchestrating a large party. Sometimes it's enough to see other people having a great time." —*DARA CAPONIGRO*

THANKSGIVING LUNCHEON

JAN SHOWERS

Photographer: JOHN CAIN SARGENT

Jan Showers is known for her impeccable taste and eye for detail. Her sense of style made her famous as an interior designer, but it has also made an incredible impact at home, now that her two daughters and granddaughter appreciate all that she does to make family meals singular experiences.

Jan's mother, Margaret Anne Smith, maternal grandmother, Hattie Boesch, and aunt Jane Noland were all big influences and taught her from a very early age the importance of entertaining well. Jan's maternal ancestors were French, and decoration, entertaining, and food were significant parts of their lives. Jan recalls amazing family dinners on Sunday with her grandmother at the helm watching over the cooking and setting the table with fine silver and gorgeous crystal and porcelain. Jan was fascinated and those scenes made a major impression on her, one that was not lost on her daughters, Susanna Showers Moldawer and Elizabeth Showers.

Susanna and Elizabeth share their mother's feeling that being together is the most important focus of a holiday, but serving correctly, placing beautiful flowers on the table, and using their treasured heirlooms are wonderful experiences too! They always mention the way

"Mom did it," referring to their grandmother, or how "Granny did it," referring to their great-grandmother at almost every family celebration.

Although every meal is treated like a special occasion at Jan's home, Thanksgiving at Jan and husband Jim's country house in Hillsboro, Texas, holds a unique place in the hearts of the Showers girls, as Jan's granddaughter, Eliza, calls them. Susanna and Elizabeth are passionate about the familiar menu that they remember their grandmother making. Jan uses a different china pattern, but the silver and crystal are the same, having been passed down to Jan and Jim. The menu is the same too: turkey, dressing, Waldorf salad, sweet potatoes, and green beans, with pecan and buttermilk pies for dessert. Yet it might be the cocktail tradition they delight in the most: champagne served on every special occasion with their signature toasted Parmesan treats.

OPPOSITE: Monogrammed linens, individual salt and pepper shakers, mother-of-pearl place cards, elegant etched crystal stemware, and Olde Avesbury by Royal Crown Derby all mix beautifully together on the Showers family's Thanksgiving table.

"My mother always said,
'Spend time on placing your
guests, as it can make or
break a dinner party.'"
—*JAN SHOWERS*

PREVIOUS OVERLEAF: A mirrored plateau down the center of
the table reflects the beautiful crystal and flowers arranged
by Jimmie Henslee. ABOVE: An ivory centerpiece bowl from
Jan's collection of vintage Jean Roger is filled with fruit and
flowers. RIGHT: Elegant white-on-white monogrammed linens
add a personal touch.
OPPOSITE: The treasured *merisier* dining table is a 1940s
interpretation of Louis XVI style. The Andre Arbus for
Seguso chandelier was found by Jan and Jim Showers on
an antique buying trip, and they gifted it to each other for
their wedding anniversary.

Jan

PARMESAN APPETIZERS

¾ cup freshly grated Parmesan cheese

½ cup mayonnaise

2 tablespoons grated onion

¼ teaspoon freshly ground white pepper

24 slices thin white bread (Pepperidge Farm Very Thin works well)

Preheat oven to 400°F. In a small bowl combine cheese, mayonnaise, onion, and pepper.

Lay bread on a work surface and cut with desired cookie cutter shapes (a circle, a turkey for Thanksgiving, a tree for Christmas, etc.).

Spread 2 teaspoons of the cheese mixture evenly onto each cutout piece of bread.

Arrange on a baking sheet and bake for 5–7 minutes, until golden and bubbly. Serve immediately.

Note: The mixture can be made ahead of time and refrigerated. You can also cut the bread ahead of time and store it in a zipper storage bag for easy preparation.

OVERLEAF: Jean Roger footed dishes (TOP LEFT) are stacked and filled with fruit and flowers to add a focal point to the table. Etched crystal (TOP RIGHT) and white porcelain tulipieres (BOTTOM RIGHT) accent the breakfast room table.

Singapore Bird plates by Adams were purchased by Jan in the 1970s in London. Jan's grandmother had the same pattern.

BOHEMIAN MIX
OF OLD AND NEW

KIM HERSOV

Photographer: INGRID RASMUSSEN

Any occasion to have a family meal together is a celebration if you have children living all around the world. As an American living abroad in England, Kim cherishes times when her family can get together and has also created close bonds with friends in England who have become like family.

Kim's grandmother, Diana Dollar Knowles, was a woman with bold, stylish flair who certainly loved a party. She entertained in different styles depending on her environment. Whether at home in San Francisco, Lake Tahoe, or Pebble Beach, her grandmother would go all out setting the table in a style that suited each home. In Lake Tahoe, she would use horn-handled flatware, which Kim inherited and now incorporates into her more bohemian table settings, mixing old and new, rustic and formal. Kim also inherited a set of china, some silver and crystal, and a set of formal silver, which she stores on an industrial rack in her kitchen.

Her grandmother might have kept her different styles quite separate, but in Kim's home everything is displayed together. Her grandmother's influence is present, and Kim says she can often "hear" her grandmother directing her preparations and table settings, as she was a stickler for details and presentation, though far from rigid. Kim, who is a stylist, has a natural flair for mixing old and new. She often uses her grandmother's formal silver chargers under her modern black-and-white porcelain plates, which were created by a selection of artists for Sarabande; one plate each is designed by Sarah Burton, Jake and Dinos Chapman, Francesca Amfitheatrof, and Ridley Scott.

Kim's love of flowers is evident as well, and she either purchases them from the corner market or orders from FlowerBX.

Another balance that Kim has mastered is creating a menu that has something for everyone. She prefers a relaxed buffet filled with both healthy options and hearty dishes so that family members can choose what they want. She is always looking for ways to make the filling English classics that her family enjoys a little bit healthier, and she is inspired by the quality, clean dishes in Mary McCartney's vegetarian cookbooks.

She sets the table with interesting items from her home, such as wooden urns and lanterns or a collection of wooden mushrooms that often make up a fall or winter centerpiece. Kim's relaxed and natural expressions of her personal style make her guests feel at home.

PREVIOUS OVERLEAF: On a black marble tabletop, Kim uses her collection of black-and-white artists plates made by Duchess China to benefit Sarabande Foundation. An embroidered napkin and a textural place mat add other artistic touches. Black and white swan salts are by L'Objet.

OPPOSITE: Modern Serpenti plates by Laboratorio Paravicini add an exotic touch to heirloom family silver service and bread plates. ABOVE: Black and white remains in focus with this modern table setting. The artists plates by Duchess China seem right at home surrounded by the art in the room, silver candlesticks, and black tapers of varying heights.

Mushroom sculptures take pride of place as a fascinating centerpiece on Kim Hersov's Thanksgiving table. Silver service plates and bread plates are from her grandmother; Laboratorio Paravicini's Serpenti plates are new.

"Set the table with interesting items from your home."

—*KIM HERSOV*

OPPOSITE: Kim enjoys a tablescape set in the secluded walled garden of her London townhome. ABOVE: Antique plates mixed with modern glassware and a pitcher of loosely arranged peonies are laid on a rustic industrial table.

OVERLEAF: Guests are welcome to make themselves at home with a refreshing cocktail or savory bites set out on the lacquered coffee table. Modern and traditional pieces mix with ease.

WEEKEND WEDDING
CELEBRATION

ALESSANDRA BRANCA

Photographers: ANA LUI & THIBAULT JEANSON

Renowned interior design- er Alessandra Branca is known for her tireless work ethic and nonstop pursuit of knowledge. Growing up in Rome, the daughter of an artist and granddaughter of an art historian, she has a well-trained eye and innate gift for finding something special in all that she is surrounded by. So how does a sought-after workhorse celebrate and relax? In great style in the comforts of the Bahamas, of course!

For Alessandra, the table is all about love—showing it and receiving it—something she has learned from all of the women in her life. She credits her mother, daughter, and daughters-in-law with showing her and constantly reminding her of this. Her home in Harbour Island, High- lowe, is full of celebrations when they are there. From small, intimate breakfasts to a big rehearsal dinner, the meals are meaningful.

The hours before family dinners are filled with a tradition that Alessandra and her grandmother started many years ago—card games! Now the late afternoons are spent playing multigen- erational games like Contract Rummy. Alessandra's entertaining mantras are "Just have fun!" and "The more the merrier." This philosophy carries through from the setup and planning to the execution of her stylish celebrations.

For a rehearsal dinner, natural chairs and a pink paisley-patterned tablecloth mix gorgeously in Alessadra Branca's Bahamian backyard.

"Just have fun.
The more the merrier!"
—ALESSANDRA BRANCA

OPPOSITE: Local colors in stripes and florals are juxtaposed
with the natural textures of rattan chargers, sea shells, and
metal lanterns.
Above: An overhead view reveals impeccable planning and
attention to detail.

In casual daytime settings for smaller parties, Alessandra's tables
delight in traditional summer colors. The effect of a cloth napkin
is indisputable.

SCRAMBLED EGGS WITH
SMOKED SALMON AND AVOCADO

8 large eggs

Himalayan salt, to taste

Freshly ground black pepper, to taste

1 avocado

4 slices of your favorite bread (Alessandra uses a homemade walnut loaf)

2 tablespoons extra virgin olive oil, plus more for drizzling

4 slices smoked salmon

Zest of 2 lemons

2 tablespoons capers

Juice of 1 lemon

Crack the eggs into a bowl, season with salt and pepper, and whisk until well combined. Set aside until ready to cook.

Peel and stone the avocado and cut lengthwise into quarters; then cut each quarter into slices.

Cover and set aside until ready to serve. Toast your favorite bread.

Using a nonstick frying pan, heat 2 tablespoons extra-virgin olive oil over medium heat. Add the egg mixture and stir continuously so the eggs cook evenly. Remember, the heat can be turned down or the pan taken off the heat if the eggs start to cook too quickly. The key to scrambled eggs is to cook slowly and evenly. They should be a creamy texture and just barely cooked; do not overcook.

To plate and serve, place a slice of toasted bread on each plate, drizzle with a little extra-virgin olive oil, add the sliced avocado and then the scrambled eggs. Top with a slice of smoked salmon, sprinkle with zest of lemon and capers, and drizzle with lemon juice. Finally, season with a little more salt and freshly ground black pepper and serve immediately.

SERVES 4

SPLENDID FAMILY MEAL

ORLENE VALY PAXSON

Photographer: AMI ROBERTSON

Orlene Valy Paxson's daughters love the daily routine of setting the table. They love to take linens from their mother's luxurious Malabar Collective line and make the table feel special yet casual. This regular habit has evolved into a ritual tradition that empowers them to take pride in their creations and create a space to make memories with their family.

Orlene grew up in Mumbai and spent summers and holidays visiting her grandmother's home on the Malabar Coast of southwestern India. Her adult life was spent between New York and Florida and now London. Spending time with her family on three different continents has shaped traditions that impact the way she strives to entertain today.

She fondly recalls watching her mother dress up for parties while she was growing up. She relates that when she was "younger in India, women would dress more elaborately than they might today for dinner parties, and fancier jewelry was the norm for such occasions."

Orlene noticed that after her mother was dressed, she would tilt her necklace a little bit to the side, making it slightly off-center. When Orlene asked about this many years later, her mother said it was important not to look too perfect. Her mother's purpose was to show the beauty in the imperfect.

For Orlene, this philosophy applies to the table and entertaining as well. She strives to make her guests feel comfortable by celebrating the little imperfections that occur naturally. She prefers natural arrangements of flowers made at home to florist-arranged bouquets, and she creates menus that are easy and fast to prepare. While her mother used pressed white linens, Orlene prefers relaxed prints. One of the family's most cherished linens is a hand-embroidered birthday table runner from India that comes out on birthdays and even travels with the family if a birthday will be celebrated away from home!

Natural light beams through Orlene's cheerful dining room set for a late spring dinner with family and friends. Orlene favors prints for her table because she worries less about stains. Layered on the block-print linen are green floral salad plates by Penny Morrison, vintage white plates, and natural place mats. Napkin rings are from Klatso. Candles are a mix of Host Home and vintage. Fragrant lilacs are arranged in a dramatic hurricane by Penny Morrison.

"Nothing should be too fussy or perfect.
This allows people to relax and be in the moment."
—*ORLENE VALY PAXSON*

ABOVE: Orlene's daughters enjoy mixing and matching linens from her Malabar collection for the table, choosing colors that suit the season.

OPPOSITE: Among things that inspire Orlene are an antique silver box from her parents' home that she has loved since childhood; a favorite picture of her mother; pictures of her children during their family travels; an antique Indian tiffin box; a lassi glass; and a bracelet she designed in her twenties, when she boldly decided to leave finance and start a fine jewelry company.

A MAXIMAL
ECLECTIC TABLE

ALLISON SPEER

Photographer: DREW ALTIZER

Allison Speer is a consummate hostess who entertains frequently. Running her own luxury public relations firm in San Francisco creates opportunities to entertain high-profile clients and dignitaries from out of town, and Allison couldn't be happier to do so.

She is exuberant about the things she has inherited and collects. Many of the women who were influential in Allison's life had a passion for collecting, and Allison has followed suit. She sets her tables with an enchanting mix of glass and china objects placed amid glorious bouquets of blooms.

Allison recalls that her mother, Susan Niven, always set a gorgeous table using the incredible roses, gardenias, and sweet peas from their garden on the table. For her Christmas tea, her mother would ask Allison to make decorated cookies and fudge, which Allison still does.

Allison remembers her step-grandmother Lucy Estelle Doheny's lavish Christmas celebrations and the tree being surrounded by gold, red, and pink boxes, caviar being served in a crystal serving set, and dogs running around everywhere. Her parties were always gregarious and fun! Allison inherited her stunning chinoiserie marquetry dining table and some exquisite dishes and accessory pieces. She entertains with a vast collection of Dresden porcelain, since both of her grandmothers collected the same pattern and some of the pieces were passed down to her.

Allison thinks of herself as more of a maximalist and is talented at designing a fascinating table mixing newer glasses and linens with her heirloom pieces for an eclectic table design. She combines vintage Imari, Murano, or Rose medallion vases for texture and likes to mix and match linens for unexpected pops of color.

When designer clients come from out of town, Allison shares San Francisco favorites by bringing in local catering from esteemed restaurants. And she feels there is always a reason to have cake! One of her favorite cakes was a replica of an Andrew Gn dress she wore at a dinner in his honor. He was thrilled and the other guests were impressed. So, whenever Andrew comes to dinner, the cake is designed after her dress for the evening.

Setting a beautiful table every day is a priority for Allison. In quieter moments, she cherishes intimate meals with her mother, where they discuss special memories of years ago that come alive through the collections on the table. From her mother, Allison learned that the perfect hostess dress is long and festive and that your smile is your best accessory.

The porcelain dishes and sterling silver flatware are inherited. The gold glasses are Murano, the linens are from Courtland and Co., and the place mats are from Mrs. Alice. OVERLEAF: Allison's grandmother's Dresden china and silver flatware are laid on the table for dinner with a custom menu card by calligrapher Barbara Callow.

10 · 19 · 2020

First Course

...hroom Soup and Truffle Oil

Second Course

...oasted Cod, Wild Mushroom Risotto
and Creamed Spinach

Dessert

Rhubarb Tart and
Surprise Birthday Cake

Ali

"Your smile is your
best accessory."
—*ALLISON SPEER*

OPPOSITE AND ABOVE: Allison adeptly blends
nontraditional objects into her tablescapes, and they
are great conversation starters.
RIGHT: Arranged over a panel of hand-painted paper
by de Gournay, Allison's inspiration board includes
photos of family and friends, a swatch of Le Tigre by
Scalamandré, and a postcard from Hotel Splendido.

129

A FIRST
BIRTHDAY

ANNABELLE MOEHLMANN

Photographer: KIRSTEN FRANCIS

Annabelle Moehlmann, founder of Land of Belle and Land of Bébé, sets the table for her daughter Clementine's first birthday.

To celebrate the occasion, Annabelle hosted an intimate tea party for her daughter with the wonderful women in her family. Romantic table linens in powder blue and soft coral acted as a backdrop for fragrant lilacs and lush peonies to take the stage at her mother's Upper East Side New York apartment. Charming floral plates by Laboratorio Paravicini played host to dazzling eats, including vibrant vegetable tarts, open-faced tea sandwiches, pansy marizpan, clementine oranges, and strawberry shortcake, all expertly made by Acquolina, Annabelle's friends and go-to caterers.

While Annabelle loves to create a beautiful mise-en-scène, she insists that a relaxed and happy environment is the key ingredient to a successful party.

Annabelle recalls a childhood filled with occasions in which raucous laughter and love were ever present.

Inspired by her mother, who is a wonderful hostess, Annabelle has her eye on important touches, such as a candle burning in the foyer, thoughtfully chosen dinnerware and table linens, lush seasonal flowers, upbeat oldies for background music, and classic cocktails (a French martini or rosé champagne are among her favorites). A few rounds of backgammon are also a welcome entertainment.

Clementine's tea party was an afternoon filled with beauty and fun. After a delicious meal, guests gathered on the floor for birthday cake and opening presents. Fun was had by all, especially Clementine. "She is a total party animal," says Annabelle, "and it makes perfect sense, as she comes from a long line of them!"

Annabelle hopes to instill in her daughter the joy that hosting loved ones can bring. Her three tried and true rules are easy to achieve: good lighting and music are key; cocktails should always be ready for guests upon arrival; and never wait too long to serve dinner!

PREVIOUS OVERLEAF: As delicious as it is beautiful, Clementine's dreamy strawberry shortcake is decorated in sweet pansies by Acquolina Catering.

ABOVE: Anabelle's mother has hosted many special occasions over the years in her lovely Upper East Side living room. OPPOSITE: A centerpiece of seasonal peonies, lilacs, and hellebores add life to the table.

OVERLEAF LEFT: A menu by The Punctilious Mr. P's Place Card Co. rests on top of a floral plate by Laboratorio Paravicini. D'Ascoli linens play host to Murano dishes holding assorted marzipan. The drinkware is by Land of Belle.

"The most important ingredient to a successful party is feeling happy and relaxed so that your guests follow suit."
—*ANNABELLE MOEHLMANN*

PRESERVING FOOD HERITAGE

ANN ITTOOP

Photographers: TRICIA COYNE, POOJA DHAR, & ANN ITTOOP

Ann Ittoop grew up in North Carolina as a first-generation Indian-American. She clearly remembers her mother's kitchen and how it combined a world of flavors representing their homes in Kerala, India, and the South. Being raised among two distinct cultures, Ann felt cooking was an important ingredient in defining her identity. She says it's what helped her bridge her multicultural upbringing.

Ann's mother, Latha Ittoop, shared a cooking principle early that continues to guide how Ann cooks today. That is, "People can *taste* what you *feel*, so make sure your mind is ready to cook." This magical lesson is what Ann now shares with her readers through recipes and food stories on her popular blog *The Familiar Kitchen*. She credits her mother for helping her feel comfortable in the kitchen and creating a strong foundation for loving the experiences that can be brought to life there. Having now grown out of her mother's kitchen, Ann finds her motivation in carrying on her family's traditional recipes so that she will never lose that connection.

OPPOSITE: Brass and gold vessels were placed on Ann's table the night before her wedding for a special Keralite ceremony called the Madhuram Veppu, where sweets were fed to her to prepare her for a sweet life ahead. Photo above by Pooja Dhar, photo opposite by Tricia Coyne.

A popular crunchy and lightly sweet Keralite snack called achappam (this page) is made with soaked rice (opposite), coconut, and a few spices, like cardamom. Photo opposite and this page by Ann Ittoop.

"My mom said that baking a cake just before guests arrive makes the home smell more welcoming, with the added bonus of getting rid of cooking and cleaning odors as well."

—ANN ITTOOP

On the morning of Ann's wedding, her mother, adorned in a bright Kerala silk saree, placed several snacks on their dining table, including rose-flavored fruit cups and rava laddus, a traditional sweet made of roasted semolina. Photos this page by Tricia Coyne, photo opposite by Pooja Dhar.

COCONUT LADDUS

2 cups freshly grated coconut

½ cup fine sooji (granulated wheat, or seminola)

¾ cup sugar

1 cup full-fat coconut milk

10–12 pods green cardamom, ground

1 tablespoon ground ginger powder

⅛ teaspoon salt

1 teaspoon ghee

½ cup desiccated coconut, for rolling

In a heavy skillet on low heat, add all ingredients except for the ghee and desiccated coconut. Continuously mix the ingredients together for about 10 minutes, or until the mixture comes together. It will look thick and will easily pull away from the pan once it's ready. Use a flat silicone spatula to flatten/smear the mixture on the pan to ensure the moisture cooks out; it makes everything hold together when there is less moisture.

Remove the pan from heat and let the mixture cool. Once it is cool enough to pick up and roll, add the ghee to your hands and roll the mixture into 1½-inch-diameter balls. Roll the balls in desiccated coconut and then transfer to a plate so they set. Once they dry, they can be refrigerated in an airtight container for up to 4–5 days.

SERVES 12–14

CHRISTMASTIME BUFFET

BETTIE PARDEE

Photographer: MOLLY LO

Bettie Pardee is such a natural hostess that you would rightly guess she has been making friends and family feel at home all of her life. She is gracious both in her personal demeanor and in her designs, whether it is touring her spectacular gardens or sitting with her on her famous Parterre Bench for a tête-à-tête. Bettie is an author and the creator of the Private Newport blog.

Parties and gatherings played a big part in Bettie's upbringing. "In my family, if we weren't planning a party, we were recovering from the last one or looking for an excuse for the next," she says. Her father "believed that friends are the greatest treasures in life" and her mother was someone who "treasured entertaining them." When Bettie was young, her parents stumbled on an idea for a new tradition, a day-after Christmas party. It was the result of a spontaneous decision to gather some friends and family around for festive fun, and it proved to be a wonderful chance to extend the holiday cheer. Bettie says her mother was a "great sentimentalist about Christmas," so the idea that this tradition would allow the season to stretch a bit further appealed to her. The Boxing Day dinner party was centered around a turkey curry, which was not only delicious but a fabulous way to use up leftovers from the traditional turkey dinner served the day before! This well-received dish became a fixture at the annual supper buffet that her parents hosted for more than thirty-five years!

Bettie still carries on her parents' tradition at her home, Parterre, in Newport, Rhode Island. She loves to bring out her mother's pair of antique, English porcelain covered dishes, one for rice and one for the curry. She also uses her mother's Royal Berlin plates for the occasion. She is more flexible now with the date, often hosting on Christmas Eve or Christmas Day instead. She has even adapted it to suit a New Year's Eve supper for six by the fire in her library.

Careful consideration and clever thought go into Bettie's party planning. She regards entertaining as an art. One of her mantras is to be persnickety: a successful party is a collection of well-tended details.

Bettie Pardee's dramatic tree can be seen from the table as it holds court in a room of its own every holiday season.

PREVIOUS OVERLEAF: Bettie Pardee's dramatic tree can be
seen from the table as it holds court in a room of its own
every holiday season.

ABOVE: A gracious Christmas welcome starts at the front door
of Bettie Pardee's Newport, Rhode Island, home.

RIGHT: Bettie uses traditional English Christmas crackers as
place cards by tying name tags to them.

OPPOSITE: The simplicity of the dining table is highlighted by
large, scalloped napkins with a graciously sized embroidered
Christmas tree, from Haute Home for Ronda Carman.

OVERLEAF: Candle glow reflects in the salon's French doors.

A LOVING TABLE

TURKEY CURRY

This recipe is a winner for so many reasons, representing comfort food at its best. Additionally, this family favorite is easy to make, cost efficient, can be doubled or tripled to serve a large group, and can be eaten with just a fork, making it a simple choice for a buffet that may require eating from one's lap. It's a good, old American recipe (long before Thai food became the rage) that has been amended to use gluten-free flour. And it freezes well, too. An added plus: the long list of condiments can make for a festive and photo-worthy presentation that will tempt even the fussiest eater.

1½ sticks butter, divided

½ cup flour (or Bob's Red Mill 1-1 Gluten-Free Baking Flour)

2–3 tablespoons curry powder

4 cups chicken broth

2 large yellow onions, chopped

2 large green apples, peeled, cored, and chopped

1 tablespoon lemon juice

Salt and pepper to taste

2 pounds cooked white turkey or chicken meat, cut bite-size

CONDIMENTS
Chutney
Chopped peanuts
Sliced scallions
Crumbled bacon
Dried raisins soaked overnight in port wine
Diced tomatoes
Toasted coconut
Diced bananas
Mandarin orange segments

CREAM SAUCE: Melt 1 stick of butter over low to medium heat; gradually add flour and whisk until smooth. Add curry powder and mix well. Cook for 2 minutes. Slowly add chicken broth, whisking continuously.

In a separate pan, sauté onions and apples in ½ stick of butter until soft. Add to curry sauce and boil until slightly thickened, stirring frequently. Reduce heat and add lemon juice, salt, and pepper to taste. Add turkey or chicken and mix well. Simmer for 1 hour.

To present, pour the curry into a deep, heated serving platter or chafing dish. Serve curry with rice, a favorite salad, and your choice of the many condiments listed below.

Cooked curry can be frozen. To reheat, place curry in an oven-proof casserole. Cover tightly. Place in a preheated 300°F oven until piping hot (about 1 hour).

SERVES 4

"In my family, we believe in pleasing friends,
welcoming them warmly, anticipating their needs, or surprising
them with something unexpected."
—*BETTIE PARDEE*

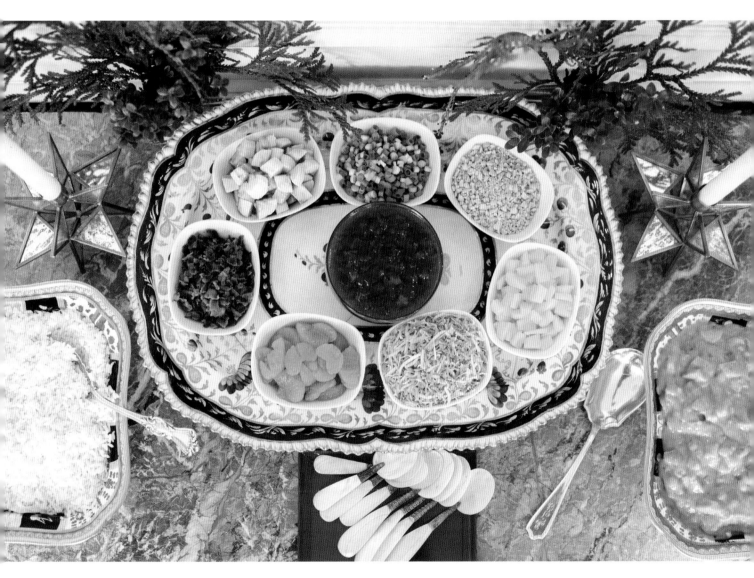

PREVIOUS OVERLEAF LEFT, TOP LEFT: A Bundt cake embellished by holiday greens was made by Bettie's head gardener, Kathleen Cotta. TOP RIGHT: Every corner is decorated with natural greens and red ribbons, including the entrance to the salon, the chandelier, and the French doors.

BOTTOM LEFT: Bettie's turkey curry is set on the salon console table. BOTTOM RIGHT: The Bundt cake is served on heirloom plates with Puiforcat silver, purchased as a gift to Bettie from her mother on their last trip to Paris together.

ENTERTAINING
WITH COLOR

FILIPA DE ABREU

Photographer: LOUIE THAIN

Even just talking about her dinner parties, Filipa de Abreu exudes the kind of enveloping energy that makes you want to be a guest in her home. She comes alive at the thought of gathering friends around the table in her sublime, mural-filled dining room.

As a brand ambassador for Tory Burch and Themis Z, among others, Filipa has plenty of opportunities to entertain. She recalls that her mother entertained formally while Filipa was growing up in London. When Filipa entertains today, she invites her children to get involved and help host at her dinners. They escort guests to their seats and even help with serving.

Filipa fills the table with beautiful objects and prefers a relaxed and laid-back ambience. For example, in addition to having the guests' names on place cards, she also adds a different quote to each one. She then asks each guest to share the quote aloud with the rest of the table. An example of one of her quotes is, "A good friend will bail you out of jail, but a best friend will be in the cell with you, saying, 'That was fun!'"

Filipa also loves monogramming and at times monograms her guests' initials on the napkins in lieu of place cards. The guests get to take the napkins home as a memento of the lovely time at her home.

One of Filipa's dinner party signatures is live music. An acoustic guitarist might play throughout dinner, or a three-piece band may make an entrance with dessert. It makes Filipa's night if her guests get swept up by the melodies and dance the night away!

ABOVE: Filipa in the back of her fiancé's Jeep filled with blue and white treasures from Tory Burch Home Collection. Location Comporta, Portugal. OPPOSITE: An easy mixture of seating options—from ballroom chairs, folding bamboo chairs, and even a pagoda daybed—make for a comfortable yet grand dining space.

OPPOSITE: The incredible murals in Filipa's Lisbon dining room were a gift from her best friend, Marie-Anne Oudejans, a Dutch-born designer based in Jaipur. The table is set with a mix of family heirlooms and new pieces found on Filipa's travels around the world.

ABOVE: A formal table of plates, silver, and glassware is grounded by a luxurious tablecloth.

ABOVE: Filipa is all smiles as she helps her guests to hors d'oeuvres
served on Portuguese cabbage ware. OPPOSITE: Filipa mixed and
matched a tabletop of treasures from around the world.
OVERLEAF: The elegant outdoor table is set in Comporta, Portugal.

THIS PAGE: An elegant al fresco tablescape in Comporta, Portugal, with handmade treasures from Greek designer Themis Z's Serenity Collection. OPPOSITE LEFT: A mix of blue and green Serenity. OPPOSITE RIGHT: A place setting of Themis Z Athenee Peacock.

"Friendship is like a muscle that needs to be exercised. It is important to continually celebrate friendship and share laughter and joy, and what better way to do that than through entertaining at home."
—*FILIPA DE ABREU*

BIRTHDAYS IN BED

CAPUCINE DE WULF GOODING

Photographer: JOHN CAIN SARGENT

The Gooding family of Charleston, South Carolina, likes to get the party started early! The family, well known for the joyful approach they take to adding beauty to our homes through their company, Juliska, starts every birthday with breakfast in bed. The entire family pitches in and each person has a special role: Dad makes breakfast, Mom makes the cake and decorates the room, and the sisters decorate the cake and dole out gifts.

But it isn't just any meal that they bring to the bedroom. A beloved family recipe for a coffee angel food cake from Capucine De Wulf Gooding's maternal grandmother, Jenny Stewart, is the ideal start to an easygoing day and a sweet way to honor the birthday person. Capucine remembers her mother making it for her when she was growing up, and now she puts this cake front and center for her family. Capucine does the baking and moves on to decorating the birthday person's bedroom, while her daughters do the cake decorating and go wild with it. Capucine likes the cake decorated with real flowers, like her mother did, but her daughters also add loads of "sprinkles and twinkles" for a unique and cheerful touch!

Breakfast, including the delightful food-face pancakes that Mr. Gooding makes, which Capucine describes as "masterpiece-ish," is served on an heirloom family tray and is topped with treasures from Juliska's pretty linens and their mouth-blown Graham pattern flutes. Of course, no celebration is complete without some sparkle, and they start the day with "kid champagne," aka sparkling fruit juice, in a grown-up glass. A toast is raised in honor of the birthday celebrant!

This family has an exuberant birthday tradition, starting each person's special day with a little pampering, laughter, and love.

PREVIOUS OVERLEAF: The makings of a thirteenth birthday celebration are gathered in one place.
ABOVE LEFT: A serving platter from Juliska's Iberian Journey collection is used to serve parfaits. ABOVE RIGHT: An heirloom tray is laden with lattes in Juliska's Berry and Thread mugs. OPPOSITE: Sparkling fruit juice is poured into toasting flutes in Juliska's Graham pattern for a breakfast toast. Flowers from the garden and heirloom silver and linens are thoughtful touches.

OVERLEAF LEFT: Funny-face pancakes are Dad's specialty.
OVERLEAF RIGHT: Capucine's family recipe for Coffee Angel Food Cake is prepared and ready for her daughters to decorate. Heirloom silver mixes with Juliska serving pieces.

"We believe that if you begin each day beautifully, the rest of
the day will follow suit. So why on earth would we wait until the end of
the day on your birthday to have cake and presents?"
—*CAPUCINE DE WULF GOODING*

COFFEE ANGEL FOOD CAKE

1½ cups sifted sugar, divided

1 cup sifted cake flour

½ teaspoon salt

1¼ cups egg whites (10–12 eggs)

1¼ teaspoons cream of tartar

½–1 teaspoon vanilla

1 tablespoon powdered instant coffee

Toasted almonds, optional

BUTTER ICING

½ cup (1 stick) salted butter, softened

¼ teaspoon salt

2½ cups sifted powdered sugar

3–4 tablespoons milk

1 teaspoon vanilla

Flavorings:

2 tablespoons powdered coffee*

2 squares melted bitter chocolate

1 teaspoon cinnamon

Preheat oven to 350°F.

In a bowl, add ½ cup sugar to the flour. Sift together four times.

In another bowl, add salt to egg whites and beat until foamy.

Sprinkle cream of tartar over egg whites and beat until soft peaks form.

Add the remaining cup of sugar, 1/4 cup at a time, to egg whites and gently fold in (use a soft spatula, always fold in same direction), about 20 strokes each time, and add the coffee and vanilla.

Now sift flour/sugar mixture into an ungreased round tube pan. Bake for 35–45 minutes.

Ice accordingly. Excellent if sprinkled with toasted almonds (a must!)

BUTTER ICING: Beat butter and add salt and sugar a little at a time. Add milk as needed and beat until light and fluffy.

*For smooth café au lait color, dissolve powdered coffee in vanilla. For speckled café color, just toss the powdered coffee in last and the micro granules leave soft speckles.

SERVES 8

Balloons, banners, and homemade gift wrapping add to the
fun of the Gooding family's birthday breakfast-in-bed tradition.

FINE & FORMAL
EVERY DAY

FRUZSINA KEEHN

Photographer: AMY NEUNSINGER

Designer Fruzsina Keehn's attention to detail and quality are evident in her fashion and in her home. From her outfits, typically from her bespoke Keehn Deutch clothing line, which she cofounded and designs for, to her jewels, always of her own eponymous line, Fruzsina's style is impeccable.

Her refined aesthetic was learned by observing her elegant mother, Veronica, whose sophisticated taste had a young Fruzsina in awe of the beauty that she created in her decorating, fashion sense, and entertaining. In the family home, every meal was eaten at the dining room table and dinners were always by candlelight. Fruzsina carries on this tradition today with her own daughter.

"My mother was a stickler for etiquette, and that certainly has had an impact on me as I always veer toward formality," Fruzsina says. At home in Beverly Hills, she takes out her finest tableware for every meal and, depending on the occasion and her mood, delights in selecting one of the patterns of several sets of the hand-painted Herend china she inherited from her Hungarian mother. Whether serving pancakes at breakfast, entertaining friends, or hosting a black tie party, she uses her finest silver and porcelain for every dining experience. She believes that, as life is a special occasion, we should use our best things every day.

Although Fruzsina doesn't enjoy cooking, she does like to make a dirty, even filthy, martini, preferring Martha Stewart's recipe that includes a blue cheese olive.

OPPOSITE: Spode Indian Tree pairs exquisitely with Buccellati bamboo-handled Tahiti flatware and Everyday Elegance linen with monograms from Monogrammit Beverly Hills.

In Fruzsina's dining room, stunning florals by Lily Lodge proprietor Ariana Lambert Smeraldo are the focal point of her elegant table.

"Use the best of what you have
every day, as life is a special occasion!"
—*FRUZSINA KEEHN*

ABOVE LEFT: The dining table is set with heirloom silver and porcelain with flowers by Lily Lodge.
ABOVE RIGHT: Fruzsina's heirloom Herend Chinois pattern.

OPPOSITE: In the living room, a drop-front secretary is set up as serving space with a Christofle ice bucket, vintage silver bar set from a trip to Paris, and gold-rimmed vintage lowballs brought home from an antique shop in London.

OPPOSITE: Heirloom silver is given new life with flowers from Lily Lodge.
ABOVE: Fruzsina's daughter, Ottavia, helps lay the table.

An intimate table set up in the library features blooming branches from Lily Lodge in a 19th-century silver vase found at auction. Buccellati fruit bowls and Schweitzer linens monogrammed by Monogrammit Beverly Hills fill the table. OPPOSITE: Herend Waldstein Rose, Tuttle Onslow silver pattern, and a Buccellati shell filled with grapes on the vine dress the library in Fruzsina's home.

BIRTHDAY IN BLUE

EMILY HERTZ

Photographer: HECTOR MANUEL SANCHEZ

Every mother's life changes the day she has a child. For Emily Hertz, an Atlanta-based home and style blogger, it was the fifth of February, the day her first child, Eloise, was born. Not only did Eloise's birthday inspire the name of Emily's popular blog Born on Fifth, but it also gave Emily an opportunity to carry on her family's tradition of marking birthdays with joyous celebrations around a family table.

Two leading ladies in Emily's life influenced the way she celebrates birthdays in her own home. Her mother always made birthdays a big deal, especially the decorations. This taught Emily to play to her strengths, so she carries on her mother's entertaining philosophy of throwing herself fully into setting a beautiful table, even if that means having to outsource the food.

She credits her mother-in-law, a storied Atlanta hostess who has organized elegant affairs for six to 600, for inspiring her to document these occasions, as she did herself. All of Emily's husband Michael's childhood birthdays were filmed in their entirety, and the family immensely enjoys watching these sentimental captures.

Her mother-in-law also started a birthday tradition of presenting a darling pre-lit ceramic cupcake at family birthday dinners. Elle looks forward to blowing out the candle, even including her little brother Jennings in the fun. This simple yet silly gesture emboldened Emily to add a touch of whimsy to each table she sets, no matter the occasion. Whether she finds little fairy figures for the children to play with or paper crackers with jokes inside, she looks for ways to add an element of surprise and delight.

In celebration of Elle's fifth birthday, Emily started an heirloom collection for the guest of honor: a set of D. Porthault Blue Coeurs linens. Emily plans to use them at all of Elle's birthday dinners and hopes that Elle will carry on the tradition with her family one day.

Though they never had the opportunity to meet, Emily credits her husband's grandmother with instilling a sense of appreciation for thoughtful celebration in him. As a family, the tradition of celebrating occasions both large and small continues from generation to generation.

PREVIOUS OVERLEAF: Emily is collecting Blue Coeurs linens from
D. Porthault for her daughter Elle's birthday celebrations, as they
fall so close to Valentine's Day. Ginori 1735's Oriente Italiano
chargers and dinner plates in pervinca are stunning with glasses
from Williams Sonoma. Flourishing place card calligraphy is
by Fleur de Letters. THIS PAGE: Emily's dining room is filled with
balloons of different shapes and sizes from MomsKloset.

ABOVE: Pum's Sweets created a four-tiered cake in blue fondant and bows. OPPOSITE: Taper candles custom painted by Sarah Gross Designs are lovely with the table runner of flowers arranged by Ginger Rose.

"It has been my greatest joy to create a treasure chest of traditions that my daughter can pass on to her family one day."
—*EMILY HERTZ*

The birthday girl in her matching Coeurs Blue dress by D. Porthault.

A FESTIVE
MEXICAN CHRISTMAS

CRISTINA LYNCH

Photographer: JOHN CAIN SARGENT

The name Cristina Lynch is synonymous with style. The dynamic duo of two generations oozes with creative energy! Cristina the first, along with her sister Jan Barboglio, started designing dresses that were a sensation in the 1980s, the Barboglio Cristina & Jan Collection. Her daughter Cristina carried on in her mother and aunt's footsteps, designing sought-after day dresses and tops highlighting the embroidery talents of artisans from Mexico, where her mother was born. Cristina the third is a baby at this writing, and her family can't wait to see where her talent and style genes take her!

Christmas is a special time for the Lynch women. They ensure that traditions provide comfort for family and friends, making their Dallas home feel like a hacienda in Mexico. One tradition that Cristina the first carries on from her childhood is La Posada. Leading up to Christmas, this is a celebration in which family and friends go from one home to another singing, and the homeowners give them something to eat or drink. Cristina likes to organize this event for her family and follows it with a buffet, the perfect way to accommodate an extra guest or two. She believes the informality allows her guests to feel free and relaxed.

Cristina the first hosts at her home and covers her beautiful table with pottery, Mexican candles, and flowers—natural accents for her traditional menu of tamales, mole, pozole, rajas, buñuelos, and a Christmas punch. She often rotates her exquisite art collection around the home, with stunning ceramics gracing her sideboards and tables when she entertains.

While growing up in Mexico, Cristina's mother always had a grand mesquite tree from the family's ranch at their home in Torreón, and people from the area would call to come by and see it.

On Christmas Day, a quiet family-only celebration ensues. They gather by the tree, decorated with framed family photos, to open their stockings adorned with charms that Cristina the first has collected on her travels and sewn onto her children's stockings every year. Now that they are grown, Cristina the second and her brother, Peter, have a new tradition of taking a tray of cheeses and a bottle of port wine to their parents to drink as the day carries on.

Cristina the second says that her mother has certainly taught her how to entertain, but mainly how to have fun! Both women have smiles and warmth that set their guests at ease.

PREVIOUS OVERLEAF AND ABOVE: Stunning florals by Stephen
Frels sit at the base of the candelabra designed by Cristina Sr.'s
sister, Jan Barboglio. OPPOSITE: Vintage Mexican chairs surround
the table. The tablecloth is by the Otomi people.

OPPOSITE, TOP LEFT: Etched glassware from Guadalajara was first used when Cristina co-chaired the Dallas Museum of Art's Beaux-Arts Ball.

TOP RIGHT: The napkins were hand embroidered by artisans in Chiapas for Mi Golondrina. BOTTOM LEFT: A tray is ready for the family cocktail tradition. BOTTOM RIGHT: Flowers by Stephen Frels fill the sculptured basket.

"One should have her party
all set and then 'arrive'
at her own party to experience
it as a guest would."
—CRISTINA LYNCH

ABOVE: Votive candles are wrapped in corn husks to give them a warm glow. OPPOSITE: Rustic and natural decor pieces are artfully arranged.

OPPOSITE: An old Saltillo serape from Cristina Sr.'s Mexican art collection is laid beneath one of her many nativity scenes from Mexico. This one is from Tlaquepaque, Jalisco. Pots of white amaryllis frame the scene.

ABOVE: Pozole is a traditional Mexican soup that Cristina loves serving for the holidays. The serving spoon is hand-carved wood from Pátzcuaro, Michoacán.

POOLSIDE
GARDEN LUNCHEON

GWEN LANGLEY

Photographer: HUNTER RYAN

Portrait by Kaitlyn Silvestri

At home in Naples, Florida, Gwen Langley loves to entertain alfresco with family and friends. She puts her kitchen skills, learned from her mother and grandmother to work and now is delighted that her own children love to cook for their family and friends. Growing up she was fortunate to be included in planning gatherings and was taught how to make the food she wanted to serve. She has successfully passed that on to her own children and says that although she didn't give intentional lessons while guiding her children around the kitchen, they are now so accomplished that she serves as their sous chef!

Gwen remembers family lunches at her grandmother's house in Miami, where aspic and cold salads were served along with fresh-squeezed juices from her grandmother's citrus trees. Gwen's mother was a talented entertainer as well. Gwen would help her mother set the table for dinner parties a day or two in advance, a habit she maintains today. She learned her mother's culinary skills by helping prepare dishes such as Lobster Thermidor, fresh shrimp salad, or fish they had caught that morning.

Gathering local flora from her own garden and adding them to her well-planned tablescapes is one of the ways that Gwen carries on the entertaining traditions she learned from her mother and grandmother. When Gwen's own daughter was young, she used to pick flowers from the backyard with her neighbors and arrange them on conch shells or in small glass votives. She would also make place cards and took the art of setting the table very seriously for a little girl! Although her daughter is now grown, Gwen carries on the tradition her daughter started and often places hibiscus flowers and a bit of greenery in shells or stalks of green bananas from her banana tree down the center of the table.

Gwen relishes any excuse to gather around a table and exuberantly plans every detail in advance, just as the women before her did. Whether the occasion was formal or casual, the women always planned menus, set their tables, and selected music ahead so that on the day of the celebration they could relax and visit with guests. They taught her, as she has taught her daughter, about the joys of entertaining friends.

"Sharing meals with your family and friends
is always a loving celebration."
—*GWEN LANGLEY*

THIS SPREAD AND OVERLEAF: Gwen's al fresco table is set with
bamboo charger plates and Mottahedeh's Carp Shell Dish, an
adaption of 17th-century Chinese export porcelain found in the
Dallas Museum of Art.

DINNER INSPIRED
BY TRAVEL

JESSICA NOWITZKI

Photographer: JOHN CAIN SARGENT

Jessica Nowitzki is at home in many parts of the world. Her childhood included time living in Sweden, Kenya, Sri Lanka, and Madagascar. She now lives much of the year in Dallas, where she works as an art consultant and, along with her husband, Dirk, blesses the city with generosity from their Dirk Nowitzki Foundation.

One priority of this busy mother of three is exposing her young children to the world that she knew growing up. The luxury of travel has been an education for the children, and Jessica makes sure that at home they get to enjoy the food traditions of places around the world that have touched her as well. She fondly recalls her mother's mastery of creating meals out of the seasonal produce.

Her mother loved to browse local produce markets and kept a greenhouse in Sweden so that she could garden year-round. Jessica says they rarely ate leftovers at home because her mother was always eager to prepare a new meal with the freshest ingredients.

As a young girl, Jessica's mother lived in a remote village in Kenya with her mother and grandmother.

When she moved to Sweden, she was taught Scandinavian traditions and was introduced to the world of porcelain. This is when she started to marry her love of cooking with beautiful vintage china. In her travels, she often bought dishes as souvenirs and would serve her favorite meals on them. Jessica treasures these dishes that have been passed down and has started collecting porcelain to add to her mother's pieces. Jessica also enjoys sourcing unique objects and florals for her table to commemorate the seasons and that relate back to her multicultural upbringing.

When Jessica entertains, she puts thought into honoring her mother's traditions. She uses ingredients that are as fresh and seasonal as possible. She keeps music playing, which reminds her of growing up in her grandmother's house with no electricity but with African music always playing from a battery-operated radio. When the batteries would die, her grandmother would sing. Like her grandmother and mother, Jessica entertains with mountains of food, plenty to drink, and an abundance of music and fun.

PREVIOUS OVERLEAF AND
THIS PAGE: Hand-crocheted
doilies from Jessica's mother
take on a new, more modern
look beneath her collection
of Nymphenburg porcelain.
Salt and pepper are offered in
pretty porcelain shells.

ABOVE: Jessica's daughter Malaika helps set the table and steals a sip of tea. OPPOSITE, TOP LEFT: Jessica's inspiration board includes her mother's necklaces from Kenya and recipes from Sweden, exotic fruit, and modern artwork. TOP RIGHT: A hand-painted glass pitcher by Lobmeyr is from Urban Flower Grange Hall.

BOTTOM LEFT: Glasses include a wine goblet by Estelle.
BOTTOM RIGHT: A tone-on-tone monogrammed hemstitch dinner napkin complements the delicate doilies.

"Unique objects for
the table commemorate
the seasons and cultural
heritage."
—JESSICA NOWITZKI

An incredible arrangement of fruit and
flowers by Urban Flower Grange Hall takes
center stage on the Nowitzkis' dining table.

A BIRTHDAY THAT
FEEDS THE SOUL

JAMIE O'BANION

Photographer: JOHN CAIN SARGENT

Jamie O'Banion is one of the hardest working women in business. As founder of BeautyBio and a leader in the beauty industry, she knows quite a bit about making things look as attractive as possible, and her priority is making people feel comfortable and adored in her home. She also knows how to celebrate!

Jamie's mother, whom she calls "her angel," began a tradition that Jamie shares with family and friends at her home in Dallas. Just as her mother does, on birthdays after the cake is served, Jamie starts out a round of short, spoken tributes in honor of the birthday person. It might be just a few quick words or a funny or sweet story. Jamie says the feeling of love and celebration is palpable during the family tradition and truly becomes the best gift of all.

Jamie's mother often said, "If not now, when, and if not me, who?" when it came to taking advantage of an opportunity to entertain. She relishes gathering family and friends for birthday celebrations. Jamie takes after her mother that way and pays attention to every detail, from the cocktail napkins to the party favors.

Blush and rose gold are Jamie's signature colors, and her birthday celebrations are a reflection of her love for any shade of pink. The cake is from Nothing Bundt Cakes; Jamie added the floral topper.

ABOVE: A loving table is set with pretty dishes, flatware, glasses, and flutes for a celebration with birthday cake. Even if it isn't a formal dinner table, Jamie lets her daughters known the occasion is special.

OPPOSITE: Jamie and her daughters love to celebrate birthdays. After the candles have been blown out, they carry on her family tradition of the "gift of words," where everyone gets to say something about the birthday person.

"Every gathering is a memory that lasts a
lifetime. When we pause and come
together our hearts and souls are fed."
— *JAMIE O'BANION*

GLOBALLY
INSPIRED TABLE

LISA FINE

Photographer: JOHN CAIN SARGENT

Portrait by Brett Wood

Lisa's personal style and fashionable approach to entertaining is a true reflection of her jet-setting lifestyle. Although she once lived in Paris, she now divides her time between Dallas and New York when not exploring other parts of the world.

She finds inspiration for her business on her global expeditions. Her textiles are printed in America and Europe but many are inspired by India. One of her favorite tablescapes is to cover the table in vintage, antique, and new pieces from her family and her travels. Italian glassware from Locchi Firenze and her inherited Francis I silver compose refined places for her friends to join her around the table. The center of the table is filled with Indian lacquer dishes holding chiles and her dramatic salt cellars were scored at an auction of Madeleine Castaing's treasures. The colors of India inspired her tablecloth, made of fabric from her eponymous line.

Lisa has truly mastered the art of a table setting that, although formal, feels very comfortable. When setting a table, her goal is to make sure that it doesn't look contrived; she prefers that they look organic and natural. She wants her flowers to look like they came from a garden, and she arranges them herself after a visit to a market or floral warehouse. She embraces the traditional elements of table design but mixes in natural elements so that it doesn't look old-fashioned. Mixing a terra-cotta pot with the finest porcelain is an example of her style.

In addition to their great style and charming Mississippi drawls, Lisa and her mother, Jean Fine, share a refined sense of appreciation for exquisite cuisine. They are both great resources for the best restaurants around the world, and when Lisa is staying with her mother, they love recreating those divine dishes at home for their friends. Lisa has a few favorite curry recipes that she adores cooking for her Southern friends and serving in a collection of antique Herend Indian Tree rimmed bowls.

Although every meal is served in style, not all are set at a formal table. Lisa often pulls out her lacquered TV trays, sets a spot for caviar and turns on a great program on-screen. She had tablecloths specially made to fit her portable trays, and the look is elegant yet casual.

Whether at a formal table or in front of a screen, dinner with Lisa is, most importantly, always filled with laughter. She makes her guests feel like cherished family. With her mother so often at the table, her meals are always full of energy and storytelling.

PREVIOUS OVERLEAF: Ranunculus in Lisa's mother's silver julep cups add pops of color. Carved horn bowls holding Indian peppers enhance with rustic beauty, while silver candlesticks nod to the traditional in this modern-traditional table setting.

ABOVE: A tablecloth made from fabric in Lisa Fine's eponymous line makes a beautiful base for her collection of vintage and new porcelain and silver found on her travels. The tablescape was inspired by a set of vintage Herend Indian Basket rimmed bowls that Lisa found online. Market-bought ranunculus, dried peppers, and kumquats add vibrant color to the center of the table.

ABOVE LEFT: The table is placed where guests can enjoy the view of Dallas's Turtle Creek. ABOVE RIGHT: Like many designers, Lisa maintains a collage of entertaining inspirations.

ABOVE AND OPPOSITE: Lisa "won" these fabulous salt cellars at the auction of the estate of Madeleine Castaing.
OVERLEAF LEFT, TOP LEFT: Lisa adeptly mixes her traditional Francis I silver with more relaxed and modern pieces. TOP RIGHT AND BOTTOM LEFT: An unusual horn spoon with a metal snail adds whimsy to the table and is ideal for using with the salt cellars.

BOTTOM RIGHT: Embroidered napkins are by D'Ascoli.
OVERLEAF RIGHT: A TV tray set up in the library is covered in a custom pink linen with service for vodka and caviar. Plates are by Carolina Irving and Daughters; glasses by Laguna B.

"I've never been
trendy but I do want
to be stylish."
—*LISA FINE*

A PASSION FOR COLLECTING

MARCIA FRENCH

Photographer: JOHN CAIN SARGENT

Marcia French's stately home in Fort Worth, Texas, has been in her family for two generations. Marcia's mother was a celebrated hostess who had a wonderful eye for tabletop treasures, and Marcia not only learned from her mother but developed the art of table setting in her own splendid ways.

Marcia has a passion for collecting tableware and can set beautiful tables in a variety of palettes and patterns using items from her extensive collections. Among her favorites is Italian-made Ernestine Salerno dinnerware, which her mother also adored. Marcia started a collection for each of her granddaughters many years ago. When they get married, she will give them the table settings she has lovingly put together.

Mixing vintage with other fabulous pieces, especially involving florals, is Marcia's style. Think vivid, hand-embroidered linens by D. Porthault framing multidimensional floral plates, colorful glassware, sparkling individual salt and peppers, and extraordinary silver. She really thinks through everything her guests might need during their time at her table.

Marcia's finesse as a hostess goes far beyond her wonderful collection of tabletop treasures, though.

She grew up in a home busy with dinner parties and luncheons hosted by her mother, whom she describes as "the most beautiful creature with the most beautiful taste." Her mother entertained frequently and with grace. She is truly an example of the concept that the more you do something, the easier it becomes. Marcia says her mother taught her by example that a very organized and thoughtful hostess will be able to take the best care of her guests. Her mother's example is seen in Marcia's attention to detail.

Marcia's granddaughters, Millicent and Annabelle, see the same qualities in Marcia. Millicent loves the way her grandmother creates memories by going "all out" with the decorations and menu. She says she can't recall a table that her grandmother has done on repeat! It is "always something new!" Annabelle recognizes that her grandmother's elegant aura makes her company feel comfortable. She is proud of the fact that an invitation to Marcia's table is always something to look forward to. This combination of grace and glamour makes memories that Marcia's guests will carry away.

PREVIOUS OVERLEAF AND ABOVE: Marcia presents a rainbow of colors in her table setting of Ernestine Salerno Pansy plates and cut crystal.

OPPOSITE TOP LEFT: The green place setting is accented with a green cut-glass goblet featuring butterflies, a silver chalice, and a pair of Artel individual salt and pepper shakers in verdure.

OPPOSITE TOP RIGHT: At every place setting, Artel salt and pepper shakers are beautiful additions.

OPPOSITE BOTTOM LEFT: Marcia thinks of every detail, including a silver lemon squeeze for her guests' iced tea.

OPPOSITE BOTTOM RIGHT: Etched butterfly stemware from Talmaris, Paris, rests on heirloom lace.

Marcia's lovely dining room is set for a family occasion.

OPPOSITE: Beaded place mats add a rich green frame to the Ernestine plates.

TOP LEFT: Marcia bought the spectacular Venetian glasses on a family trip in the 1970s.

TOP RIGHT: One of a pair of Chinese figures that belonged to Marcia's parents is now used on her tablescape.

RIGHT: Embroidered linens by D. Porthault pull the touch of yellow from the floral arrangements.

OVERLEAF LEFT: Hand-embroidered table linens by D. Porthault look as if they were custom made for Marcia's collection of Ernestine. Real flowers and four porcelain Boehm roses are handsomely combined.

OVERLEAF RIGHT, TOP LEFT: Embroidered linens by D. Porthault sit atop a vintage plate by Ernestine.

TOP RIGHT: Porcelain floral salt and peppers and place card holders are placed at each seat.

BOTTOM LEFT: A mix of elements results in a gorgeous color scheme.

BOTTOM RIGHT: Marcia's mother's serving table was frequently used for caviar and hors d'oeuvres. Today, Marcia uses it for tea and coffee service.

"I learned from my mother's example that a very organized and thoughtful hostess will be able to take the best care of her guests.
—MARCIA FRENCH

AN EXOTIC
DINNER

MAURA KENT

Photographer: USCHI IRANI

In a home away from home, Maura Kent has embraced the exotic traits that define life in Dubai. From Saudi Arabian dates and Lebanese chocolates on her coffee tray to little brass camels picked up in the souk, she celebrates the things that make her life in the Middle East unique. Her mother encouraged her travels and Maura has lived in many different countries. However, inspiration still springs from her childhood in Ireland. She says there is no doubt that her love of setting a nice table comes from her mother.

Her mother loved Irish linen napkins, Irish silver, and Irish crystal on the table for special occasions. She was very traditional and, because she was a busy working mother, she kept her tables simple and never veered from her white linens and treasured crystal and silver.

Maura continues to care deeply about where her plates, cutlery, and linens are made, but she has a strong preference for artisanal or small, family-owned brands. While she loves Irish linen, she prefers unique colors to her mother's white. Maura also uses patterns and likes to experiment with decoration by picking up objects and textiles on her travels and adding them to the tablescape.

Maura has a special love for the Middle East and its cultures. She explains that "hospitality is a strong Irish trait, and Arabs are incredibly hospitable people too." She continues, "Hosts in both countries share a desire and an ability to make their guests feel very welcome and cared for." Although she thinks fondly of Ireland, a country steeped in traditions and hearty meals, she prefers to celebrate with simple food—salads, grilled fish, or a one-pot vegetarian dish, and chocolate cake from a local bakery.

Maura's mother was also an avid gardener who kept simple arrangements of fresh flowers around the house, and Maura does the same. Happily for Maura, her daughters show a lot of interest in her dinner party preparations and take pride in setting a table themselves for her birthday or Mother's Day.

Maura Kent lights the candles and prepares for guests at her palm-filled home in Dubai. Brass candlesticks by Caravane, camels from the souk in Dubai, and vases from a shop in Madrid add another layer of elegance to Maura's exotic table.

An animal-print tablecloth by L'Objet steals the show on Maura's buffet. The brass tray is from Nada Debs, the brass bowl is by Kafka Goes Pink, and the cake plate is by Cabana.

"Like my mother, I like to know where my plates, cutlery, and table linens were made and I have a strong preference for artisanal or small family-owned brands."
—*MAURA KENT*

OPPOSITE: Cabbage ware from Bordallo Pinheiro and Serpenti hand painted plates from Laboratorio Paravicini mix and match alongside brass accents and glassware from R+D Lab and Crate & Barrel. The brass flatware is Cutipol.

TABLES FOR EVERY OCCASION

MEGAN STOKES

Photographer: JOHN CAIN SARGENT

Now a young Charleston style-setter, Megan Stokes was raised in a family that offered guests a gracious welcome, in the way of many Southern hostesses. Megan's mother has been a great influence on the way she entertains today. From the way her mother would make a simple burger night more special for her family by always whipping up chocolate milkshakes to go with them or the extraordinary number of balloons she would cover the room with on birthdays, Megan looks back on childhood special occasions with a smile. She also admires that her mother is the type of hostess who can find out with an hour's notice that ten people are coming for dinner and be ready to greet them with hors d'oeuvres, dinner, and a smile.

Megan knows how to create beautiful spaces in great Charleston style, using pieces inherited from her family. She especially values the pieces passed down from her grandmother, such as her memie's green water goblets and sterling silver flatware. She makes place for these at many a table. She also carries on a cherished box cake recipe that her grandmother made for her mother's birthday every year. She fondly remembers during visits to her grandparents' home eating desserts, much like this strawberry cake, for breakfast at the kitchen table while her grandmother would sip her tea and read the morning paper.

Owning several sets of dishes allows Megan to set lovely tables for many occasions or no occasion at all. Even if pizza is on the menu, Megan still sets the table and lights the candles.

What does she hope to pass along to her children? Certainly a craving for Memie's Strawberry Cake for breakfast on their birthdays is on the list as well as that magic touch that makes the little things feel special. Most important, her mother always has a way of making her guests feel loved and Megan strives to entertain that way and hopes to see her children do the same someday.

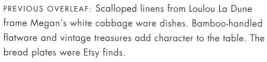

PREVIOUS OVERLEAF: Scalloped linens from Loulou La Dune
frame Megan's white cabbage ware dishes. Bamboo-handled
flatware and vintage treasures add character to the table. The
bread plates were Etsy finds.

RIGHT: Megan's grandmother's vintage stemware looks
modern paired with candlesticks from The Avenue.

OVERLEAF: A simple arrangement of *Gypsophila* (baby's
breath) gives Megan's dining room an ethereal look.
Indian block-print linens from Julia Amory are paired with
Herend Princess Victoria, Megan's wedding china. The gold
chargers are by Vietri and the silver flatware was Megan's
grandmother's Old Masters pattern, which was passed on
to Megan.

"A good playlist is the key to setting the mood!
I have songs on queue for every occasion."
—*MEGAN STOKES*

On her porch in Charleston, Megan uses an Indian block-print
tablecloth by Julia Amory. Plates are from Vietri.

BRINGING
THE OUTSIDE IN

PENNY MORRISON

Photographer: MIKE GARLICK

Admired interior designer Penny Morrison likes to make a big effort dressing her tables for all occasions big and small. She adores a relaxed lunch with friends and especially loves to entertain in the spring or summer, when spirits are uplifted and there is much more scope for delicious fresh meats and salads. Penny tries to bring the outside in with lots of fresh flowers, open doors, and making the most of glorious views across the valleys surrounding her home in Wales.

Influenced by her mother while growing up in South Africa, Penny says the tradition of laying the table correctly remains very important to her. She does things in a similar way to her mother but prefers to use more layers on the table. She remains inspired by her mother's meticulous way of keeping her house neat and feeling fresh.

She loves collecting vintage textiles and sets of china, whether from an auction or her own designs. Her Penny Morrison collection of pretty painted ceramic tableware was launched a few years ago and is a wonderful mix with some of her classic antiques.

Penny has always valued the importance of sitting down at a table and eating together with family and friends. Laying the table with flowers is a tradition she cherishes because it makes the home both welcoming and inspiring. Whether they eat inside or outside, she believes that, in the evening, as many candles as possible should be used to create ambiance and atmosphere. Pretty glassware filled with delicious wine is important too!

She also likes to serve a variety of foods from different countries and cultures because she finds that everyone enjoys trying something unique. One of Penny's special dishes is her Smoked Haddock Casserole. She lays portion-size pieces of undyed smoked haddock in a casserole dish covered with heavy cream, minced shallot, and thyme, with Parmesan sprinkled on the top. It goes into the oven for 30 minutes and is served with black wild rice and green salad. It's so easy, she says, and everyone loves it.

Penny's mantra is to have everything ready to go before a party so that she can look organized and enjoy herself!

A blue and white tulip tablecloth, Pink and Blue Summer Flower
Ceramics, Green and Pink Marbled Ceramic Pudding Bowl, and
an Aubergine Cylinder Glass Hurricane Lamp filled with flowers
are all from Penny Morrison's eponymous collection.

"It's all about creating a space of feeling and unique personality.
There is no right or wrong."
—*PENNY MORRISON*

PREVIOUS OVERLEAF: Dramatic Green Glass Thumb Cut Hurricane
Lamps are filled with flowers, while Green Summer Flower
Ceramic Large Plates are laid on a table with heirloom linens and
silver.
ABOVE: A tablecloth made from Simla Blue and Green is topped
with a natural wicker place mat and Green Summer Flower
Ceramics from Penny's eponymous collection.
OPPOSITE TOP: Penny's hand-painted ceramics in Blue Palm Tree
mix cheerily with traditional fabrics, a classic scalloped napkin, a
wicker place mat, and heirloom silver.

OPPOSITE BOTTOM: Penny's hand-painted ceramics in Green Palm
rest on a tablecloth in shades of pink and a wicker place mat.
OVERLEAF: The Aleppo Cinnamon Tablecloth by Penny Morrison
is mixed with place mats from Colombia and Penny's collection of
Green Marbled Ceramics.

257

Penny Morrison's table is set with her Aleppo Blue Tablecloth with Peach Large Flower reversible place mats. Stunning Green and Champagne Diamond-Cut Hurricane Lamps will make the candlelight glimmer. Taper candles and Speckled Ceramics from Penny's collection add a relaxed element to the formal dining space.

AN ARTISTIC TABLE

SHARON LEE

Photographer: JOHN CAIN SARGENT

Sharon Lee grew up with a mother she refers to as a "Renaissance woman." Her mother, Jane Lee, is a dedicated mother of three, grandmother of four, concert pianist and organist, master florist, opera singer, and an accredited Korean folk art painter. She also heads up her women's group, Korean American Muse, of which Sharon is a part. It's no wonder she is an inspiration to her daughter. Sharon shares her mother's artistic talent. She is a celebrated fine artist, interior designer, and the founder of Krane Home, which features home products created from her original artwork.

When it comes to entertaining, Sharon finds inspiration in her mother, sister, and friends. Her mother's incredible floral creations are often full of meaning. Their favorite flower is the peony, not only for its beauty but because it symbolizes abundance and prosperity in Korean art. Sharon's favorite room in her Dallas home is the dining room, where her guests dine on the very antique table and chairs that she grew up with.

Sharon's sister, Greta Lee, is also a creative force and inspiration to her. As an actress and writer Greta is described as "hardworking," but as a hostess she has a "magical ease." Sharon also finds inspiration in her girlfriends, each of whom brings something to the table. She has taken something away from every dinner she has been to, says Sharon, whether it is going around the table sharing a favorite memory with the host, sprinkling sequins or candy around the table for decor, making home-grown floral arrangements, embracing a fun theme for no reason, adding a girly party favor, or bringing a gift to be donated to a cause.

Sharon's mother also taught her to make a fruit platter whenever she entertains, no matter what the occasion. Sharon states, "Fruit is colorful and pretty already, so it's easy to arrange on a plate. A pineapple top looks impressive in the center. My mother taught me to garnish it with simple garden cuttings like camellia leaves. Koreans absolutely love fruit. It is common in our culture to bring over an entire box of pears or melons as a hostess gift!"

PREVIOUS OVERLEAF AND RIGHT: Sharon Lee makes a
vibrant and fun place for a family meal in her dining
room. Palm Tree Candlesticks are from ShopKSW. Green
glassware is by La Rochere; etched glasses are designed by
Artel. All textiles are designed by Sharon for Krane Home.
ABOVE: Mottahedeh Blue Lace and Famille Verte patterns
layer splendidly with hand-embroidered, scalloped place
mats designed by Kimberly Schlegel Whitman for Elizabeth
Lake and napkins custom made by Sharon Lee in textiles
from her Krane Home line.

OVERLEAF LEFT: Sharon arranged peonies, berries, and hydrangeas in a vintage footed bowl for the center of the table.

OVERLEAF RIGHT, TOP LEFT: Palm Candlesticks by ShopKSW. TOP RIGHT: Verdure Salt and Peppers by Artel. BOTTOM LEFT: A mix of glassware by La Rochere and Artel. BOTTOM RIGHT: A vintage swan Sharon found on an antiquing outing with her mother.

"Make a fruit platter
whenever you
entertain, no matter
what the occasion."
—*SHARON LEE*

KOREAN RICE CAKES SERVED WITH HONEY

Sharon's mother would make these, sometimes even for breakfast! They're a lot of fun at a party because they're paired with honey for dipping. It makes a cute tray-passed dessert.

1 cup rice flour

½ cup hot water

17–18-ounce container of sweet red bean paste

Sesame oil

Nutmeg

Honey for dipping

To make dough, mix rice flour with water and knead in a bowl until smooth. Form into a disk.

Create 1-inch-diameter balls of dough and press down in the center to form a well. Scoop 1 teaspoon of the red bean paste into the center of each and form the dough around it. Mold each ball into a half-moon shape.

Heat 1 teaspoon sesame oil in a frying pan on low heat. Pan-fry the half-moon cakes until cooked through and golden brown on each side.

Sprinkle with nutmeg. Serve with honey for dipping.

MAKES 20 PANCAKES

ABOVE: Sharon's modern sideboard is covered in traditional Korean treats. The small paintings on the sideboard are also hand painted by Sharon.
OPPOSITE TOP: Traditional Korean desserts are displayed in a Blue Lace Scalloped Bowl by Mottahedeh.
OPPOSITE BOTTOM: Korean rice cakes are beautifully presented.

A MOTHER-DAUGHTER LUNCHEON

STEPHANIE BOOTH SHAFRAN

Photographer: THE INGALLS

As a fifth generation Angelino, Stephanie Booth Shafran grew up in a home where her parents frequently entertained a wide circle of friends. Her mother was passionate about making every gathering special, and Stephanie inherited her love of entertaining. She is now one of Los Angeles's preeminent hostesses and author of her own book on entertaining.

Stephanie has fond memories of being in the garden with her mother cutting roses for the table before a dinner. Today, Stephanie grows the same roses in her own garden and loves to use them around the house and on the tabletop when entertaining. She inherited classic and elegant silver, crystal, and china from her mother and, while she maintains the tradition of using these pieces, she prefers to combine them with more modern elements to showcase her own unique style. She understands that the beauty of the tablescape is not in each individual piece on the table but about how they are put together to create an overall look.

One of her entertaining principles is that parties are not about perfection. They are about joy! Stephanie's tables look perfect in her pictures, but she knows that the truly memorable moments come from the little snafus and authentic moments that are bound to happen, no matter how much a hostess has prepared for her guests. She also credits her father's adage "Do it now" for its wonderful reminder that there is no time like the present to celebrate.

OPPOSITE: Blue and white porcelain by Marie Daâge is perfectly placed on an apple green tablecloth. Pink glasses were rented to add a pop of whimsical color, and the wine being served is placed on a crystal coaster by Baccarat.

OPPOSITE AND ABOVE: Meticulously aligned place settings make
the tables stylish, while centerpiece arrangements of green
hydrangeas amidst collections of white, single-variety bouquets
heighten the refinement.

AVOCADO GAZPACHO

2 extra-large or 3 large, ripe avocados, halved,
  pitted and peeled

1 Persian cucumber, cut into quarters

1 green onion, trimmed, cut into pieces

3 tablespoons fresh lemon juice

Pinch of black pepper

Pinch of red pepper

3 cups chilled chicken broth

GARNISH OPTIONS

Chopped cooked lobster, shrimp, or crab

Cherry tomatoes, quartered

Cilantro leaves

Plain yogurt

Extra-virgin olive oil

Sliced green onion

Sliced radishes

Combine avocados, cucumber, green onion, lemon juice, and black and red pepper in a heavy-duty blender. Add chicken broth and blend until very smooth. Season the soup to taste with salt. Refrigerate the soup until well chilled, about 1 hour. (Soup can be prepared up to 4 hours ahead; keep refrigerated.) Pour the soup into bowls; dividing evenly. Garnish as desired and serve.

SERVES 6

OPPOSITE: Elegant silver flatware from Christofle and plates by Marie Daâge frame lovely salmon salads.
ABOVE: Avocado Gazpacho with pretty garnishes appeals to the eye first.

"Parties are not about perfection. They are about joy!"
—*STEPHANIE BOOTH SHAFRAN*

OPPOSITE TOP LEFT: Stephanie lays out her silver flatware, inherited from her mother. TOP RIGHT: Topiary cocktail napkins are folded and ready for guests. BOTTOM LEFT: An elaborate three-color monogram ties together some of the celebration colors. BOTTOM RIGHT: Hot-air balloon place cards found on Etsy are nestled in silver frog place card holders by Ercuis.

ABOVE LEFT: White flowers in blush vases are ready to be set on the table alongside stacks of plates by Marie Daâge. ABOVE RIGHT: Vintage white tulipieres hold pink flowers. BELOW RIGHT: A champagne bucket by Simon Pearce holds a bottle of rosé. Garden roses in Baccarat vases perfectly match the color of the summer wine.

OVERLEAF LEFT: Joyful colors greet guests at the dessert table, covered in hot-air balloon fabric by Manuel Canovas. The vibrant purple plates from Haviland frame sweet key lime tarts.

OVERLEAF RIGHT, TOP LEFT: The dessert table wows with a dramatic arrangement of purple blooms in a vase by Aerin Lauder. TOP RIGHT: A feminine cake is decorated with roses. MIDDLE RIGHT: An heirloom silver tray Stephanie inherited from her mother holds refreshments and embroidered ballerina cocktail napkins by Julia B.

FESTIVE LUNCH IN THE GARDEN

NATALIE STEEN

Photographer: STEPHANIE MAS
Set Designer: CECILE GARCIA / Hair & Makeup: LUTZ KARPF

As a Cuban-American who hasn't herself been to the country her family emigrated from, Natalie Steen values its cultural traditions and is weaving them into the lives of the next generation.

Because of the example of hard work and tenacity in her family, Natalie honors them by doing everything to the best of her ability. She constantly reminds herself that "a sense of belonging is a blessing," observing that "to be able to offer that to another in the form of kinship and hospitality is one of the greatest gifts you can give."

Natalie practices law in Houston, and her creative side comes to life with her weekly fashion-focused newsletter called *The Nat Note*. She has moved to Texas, away from her family in Miami and the home she grew up in, but she sees every return visit as an opportunity to catch up with old friends over a casual lunch or dinner party in her parents' backyard overlooking the Coral Gables waterway. During the winter months, it is the perfect spot for al fresco entertaining.

She incorporates details that personalize the table and provide great conversation starters. She gets the party started with a curated playlist to set the mood.

While Natalie's strengths do not lie in the kitchen, she loves to plan a festive menu. A favorite is her grandmother Olga's recipe for *Flan de Coco* (Coconut Flan) from *Cocina Criolla* by Nitza Villapol, a 1950s-era Cuban cookbook. She fondly recalls being a young girl on a step stool in the kitchen next to her grandmother, trying to get a good look at the stovetop and being mesmerized as the white sugar caramelized into a golden-brown syrup to form the flan topping.

It isn't just the heirlooms and recipes that Natalie gives life to. It is also the axiom that the women in her family often repeat aloud, *"Vísteme despacio que estoy de prisa"* ("Dress me slowly because I am in a hurry")—a reminder to take your time to avoid forgetting something important. Natalie believes this accounts for something known as "Cuban time," where everyone is typically running fifteen to thirty minutes late for everything—which makes an opportunity for the hostess to have a pre-party cocktail!

Although she is a big advocate of getting the most use out of one's treasured pieces, Natalie knows these are not the most important ingredient to a good party. "No, you shouldn't let dust gather on your wedding china, but you also shouldn't be surprised if a meal shared over paper plates ends up being one for the books."

PREVIOUS OVERLEAF AND PAGE 279: Tablecloth by India Amory and napkins by Cabana Canary are layered with place mats and cocktail napkins by Verannia.

LEFT: In Natalie Steen's mother's Miami backyard, festive colors and prints set the tone for a fun-filled luncheon that Natalie refers to as "happy chaos." Bordallo Pinheiro Cabbage ware plates, porcelain flowers and birds, and printed napkins and tablecloths all mix delightfully together. In a nod to her maternal grandmother, Natalie has used the small sterling silver ashtrays that her grandmother was able to bring from Cuba as salt and pepper cellars. Place card calligraphy is by Laura Lines. ABOVE: Natalie's inspiration board.

OVERLEAF LEFT, TOP LEFT: Cabbage ware tureen by Bordallo Pinheiro. TOP RIGHT: The porcelain birds were an estate-sale find. BOTTOM LEFT: Mojitos are served in a wicker-wrapped decanter and matching glasses. BOTTOM RIGHT: Bread is kept fresh in a Los Steens embroidered napkin by Coley Home.

"Life is too short and
too unpredictable
not to celebrate
life's moments with
those you love."
—NATALIE STEEN

100TH BIRTHDAY
FOR GRANDPA

CLARY BOSBYSHELL WELSH

PHOTOGRAPHER: CATMAX PHOTOGRAPHY

There is no occasion quite a special as the celebration of a 100th birthday! For the Bosbyshell family, celebrating their patriarch, Bob, called for a backyard family gathering. The guest of honor was celebrated with personal touches created thoughtfully by his granddaughter, interior designer Clary Bosbyshell Welsh. Clary's goal was to create a table that would be filled with her grandfather's favorite things so that every family member there would take home wonderful memories. The backyard of her Atlanta home was the perfect setting.

One special way to honor a guest is to serve a menu of their favorite foods. Bob Bosbyshell grew up in San Antonio, Texas, so, naturally, his favorite dishes had a Tex-Mex flare. The menu included chicken enchiladas and homemade margaritas. The menu cards were hand drawn by Clary's mother-in-law, Susan Churchill. Susan also happens to be Clary's mother's best friend since childhood!

The tablescape on the deck was set with family heirlooms augmented with Clary's fresh touch. She loves to put her own spin on the tablescapes of generations before her. Although she collects the same china as her mother, Mottahedeh's Sacred Bird and Butterfly, she likes to mix it with other patterns or use potted plants in place of floral arrangements. In this case, Clary also incorporated her maternal grandmother's silver flatware and her paternal grandmother's silver candlesticks. She used monogrammed napkins from her own wedding to her husband, Graham.

Clary comes from a long line of devoted tablescape lovers. Her great-grandmother, grandmother, and mother all carried on the tradition of setting a beautiful table for every meal. Clary remembers that her mother, Margaret, set the table every night when she was growing up, whether it was a Monday night family dinner or a black-tie affair. She always pulled out the finest china and linens. Clary often uses table linens that she collects on her travels as a memory of the places she has been.

Personal touches like these are wonderful ways to honor family.

PREVIOUS OVERLEAF: A place setting worthy of the special occasion was styled by Clary using Mottahedeh Sacred Bird and Butterfly pattern, which both she and her mother collect. The monogrammed napkins were made by Gramercy Home for Clary's wedding and wonderfully match the custom Loulou La Dune scalloped place mats. Etched glasses are from Williams Sonoma. Menu cards were hand drawn by Clary's mother-in-law, Susan Churchill. Flourish place cards were hand drawn by Fleur de Letters. The silver candlesticks belonged to Clary's grandmother. The floral tablecloth was rented from Freshly Set.
OPPOSITE AND TOP RIGHT: Roses and ranunculus were designed by Mary Delia Gaines in small arrangements and placed down the center of the table.
BOTTOM RIGHT: Clary and her daughter enjoy a loving moment with Grandpa Bob.

"Hosting is always
about having fun,
not taking it all to seriously!
It is a party, after all!"
—*CLARY BOSBYSHELL WELSH*

TOP LEFT: A special chocolate birthday cake was presented on heirloom silver. TOP RIGHT: A detail of the Sacred Bird and Butterfly pattern by Mottahedeh. Silver flatware is from Clary's mother's collection. BOTTOM RIGHT: Elegant silver salt and pepper shakers were laid on the table.

ACKNOWLEDGMENTS

We are truly grateful for the incredible and talented women featured in this book. Without them, *A Loving Table* would not have been possible. Their willingness to share the special moments and traditions captured on these pages shows their unique and authentic loving table. Thank you!

To Mark D. Sikes, thank you for the personal and heartfelt forward to this book and for appreciating beauty and the feelings it evokes.

Thank you, Jennifer Gracie and Gracie Studio, for allowing us to use your incredible design on the end sheets.

Special thanks go to the many amazing and accomplished photographers who collaborated with us. Your eye for beauty and your ability to bring to life these magical settings, highlighting these lovely women in their homes, are a truly gifts for all to enjoy. An extra special thanks to John Cain Sargent, who so easily captures the beauty around him at every event he photographs.

To our editor, Madge Baird, and everyone at Gibbs Smith, we cannot thank you enough. To our book designer, Rita Sowins, thank you for making it so beautiful!

To our agent, Kari Stuart, and your support team at ICM, thank you for your leadership and wisdom.

To our readers, we hope these pages inspire you to create and cherish your own traditions and memories around a loving table.

KIMBERLY & SHELLEY

I personally thank you, Kimberly, for bringing me along on this adventure. You are an incredible woman with such grace, kindness, and talent, and this project would not have been possible without you. I am honored to call you my friend and now coauthor!

Thank you, Sandi Rupprecht, for your critical role in keeping us all organized. Your friendship over the years has meant the world to me, and I am happy to have you by my side.

To my parents, thank you for showing me a world where you notice and appreciate the details and you stop and smell the roses. I will forever cherish the effort you've made in passing these values and traditions on to me.

To my husband, Brett, thank you for your love and support. To our children, Hunter, Ford, Will, Luke, and Lauren; our daughter-in-law, Sophie; my sister, Mindy; and all my extended family and friends, thank you for being my loving table—a special place where beautiful memories are created and shared.

XX SHELLEY

To Shelley, it was such a treat to get to work with you on this book. You are so talented, and I have enjoyed every minute of this project, from our initial coffee when the idea sparked until now!

I don't know how I would get through a day without Maddy Critz! Thank you for all that you do to keep things running as smoothly as possible. Your heart for the Lord and your kind and generous spirit are a delight to be around every day.

Thank you to Ellen Wilkerson and Michael Bentley for all of your support. It is much needed and greatly appreciated!

To my parents, thank you for always being so supportive and for teaching me that every day should be a celebration. You have truly taught all of us that there is value in our heritage, that traditions are meaningful, and that there is always room at the table for more.

To my mother-in-law, Caroline, thank you for sharing your family's traditions and French customs with me so that I can keep them going with your son and grandchildren.

Thank you to my entire extended family for always being up for a celebration! From our wild Easter egg hunts to dressing up and learning lines for a Christmas Nativity play. You are all such great sports!

To Justin, JR, and Millie, your unwavering support of all of my projects means the world to me. I pray that you will always make time around the loving table with family a priority. I am grateful for you, and I love you so much.

GRATEFULLY,
KIMBERLY

PHOTOGRAPHIC
CREDITS

Drew Altizer, 122–29

Catmax Photography, 290–97

Tricia Coyne, 137, 140

Pooja Dhar, 136, 141

Donna Dotan, 14–21

Kirsten Francis, 130–35

Mike Garlick, 252–61

Tria Giovan, 46–51

Alison Gootee, 28–35

Gracie Studio, end sheets

Holt Haynsworth, 62–67

The Ingalls, 270–79

Uschi Irani, 236–43

Anne Ittoop, 138–39

Thibault Jeanson, 104, 110BR, 112–14, 115TM, 115ML, 115MM, 115MR, 115BL, 115BM

Kevin Kerr, 302R

Cynthia Lynn Kim, 5, 36–45

Max Kim-Bee, 78–81

João Lima, 68–77

Molly Lo, 142–51

Ana Lui, 105, 106–109, 110TL, 110TR, 110BL, 111, 115TL, 115TR, 115BR

Stephanie Mas, 280–89

Hunter Mitchell, 22

Nam Dang-Mitchell, 23–27

Amy Neunsinger, 170–79

Ingrid Rasmussen, 94–103

Ami Robertson, 116–21

Hunter Ryan Photo, 2, 199–205

Hector Manuel Sanchez, 180–87

Kaitlyn Silvestri Photography, 198

John Cain Sargent, 8–9, 13, 52–61, 82–93, 162–69, 188–97, 206–35, 244–51, 262–69, 298, 300, 302, 303L

Louie Thain, 152–61

Brett Wood, 218

PREVIOUS OVERLEAF: Image from Sharon Lee, page 262.
OPPOSITE: Image from Cristina Lynch, page 188
OVERLEAF: Image from Lisa Fine, page 218.

THE AUTHORS

Photo by John Cain Sargent

Photo by Kevin Kerr

KIMBERLY SCHLEGEL WHITMAN is an author, lifestyle expert, TV and radio personality, social media aficionado, blogger, and founder of ShopKSW.com. She regularly appears on television programs, including NBC's *Today* and *Access Hollywood*. She is the author of eight other books on entertaining, among them *Tablescapes: Setting the Table with Style*, *Monograms for the Home: The Art of Making Your Mark*, *The Pleasure of Your Company: Entertaining in High Style*, and *The Wedding Workbook: A Time Saving Guide for the Busy Bride*. She is an ambassador for NorthPark Center in Dallas, where she lives with her husband, Justin; son, JR; daughter, Millie; and Giant Schnauzer, Zeus. You can follow along as she shares daily lifestyle inspiration on social media at @KimberlyWhitman.

SHELLEY JOHNSTONE PASCHKE is an interior designer with a studio and showroom in Lake Forest, Illinois. She has been nationally recognized for her signature, elegant European-influenced interiors with a fresh, modern twist. Shelley has been featured in *House Beautiful*, *Traditional Home*, *Veranda*, *Luxe*, the *New York Times*, *ArchDigest.com*, and *Tory Daily*.

Shelley's luxury boutique design firm creates beautiful and timeless spaces for her clients to enjoy. She resides in Lake Forest and Naples, Florida, with her husband, Brett. They are parents to Hunter, Ford, Will, Luke, Lauren, daughter-in-law Sophie, and eighteen-year-old West Highland Terrier, Adler. You can follow Shelley on social media at @shelleyjohnstonedesign.